Awakening to God

Not a Man in the Sky

Awakening to God
Not a Man in the Sky

ALICE ROST

Night Star Publisher
San Diego, California

NIGHT STAR PUBLISHER
San Diego, California

Printed in the United States

print ISBN: 978-1-929909-11-7
eBook ISBN: 978-1-929909-12-4

Book and Cover Design
Jan Carpenter Tucker
www.nightstarpublisher.com

Production Notes
These fonts were used in the design of this book:
Carlton • Great Vibes • Adobe Garamond Pro family
Dreamy woman original artwork: www.logoopenstock.com
Graphic elements: vecteezy.com

Acknowledgments

Thank you Holos University staff for the care you took with shepherding me through my graduate coursework with care and consideration.

Thank you Bob Nunley for "getting me" and understanding my project long before I did. You said the magic words... "It is all personal and why don't you use yourself as a case study?" I knew those words were bingo, but it took me a full year to step into them. My gratitude runs deep and although you are no longer here in body, I'm fairly certain you have received this message.

Thank you Sandy Augustine for the best friendship and partnership anyone could imagine.

Thank you Emily Hanlon. Your friendship and coaching long ago gave me the tools to write with some coherence.

Isabella Furth edited this book, untangling awkward phrasing and clarifying what I obscured. Jan Carpenter Tucker designed the book and created a physical version I could never have imagined.

Thank you Jerry Rost for not only financing me and supporting my work, but for joining me on this amazing spiritual journey. How brilliant that we can do this together side-by-side looking in the same direction.

TABLE OF CONTENTS

Introduction

This book is a personal journey fueled by scholarship. Approximately five years ago, when I began my graduate studies at Holos University, I was interested in gaining scholarly knowledge that would enhance my connection to spirit. My interests were in spirituality, holistic health and (I thought at the time) transpersonal psychology. As a secular Jew, raised on the streets of working-class Brooklyn, I early on chose the path of materialism and, although I had a slight impression that I was spiritually connected, my worldview largely excluded spirit. Karl Marx said, "Religion is the opiate of the people," and Friedrich Nietzsche offered the oft-repeated, "God is dead." That sounded pretty good to me. If I was unable to see it, hear it, touch it, smell it or taste it, it wasn't worth investigating. I chose to ignore the persistent tap on my shoulder telling me that there just might be more.

And yet, by my late sixties I was pursuing a graduate degree in theology and doing so with a passion I had no idea existed. What happened? All those years when I disregarded sacred music that pulled at my heart, when beauty seemed almost too much to bear, when I just knew something to be true, but had no idea how I had obtained the knowledge, when I experienced a divine connection and then discarded it for lack of understanding, when I entered a church or synagogue for some kind of celebration and immediately tears filled my eyes—all these feelings were easily brushed aside. And yet they persisted.

Two things set me on the path of developing my personal theology. First, I got sick. Just eight years after breast cancer surgery and treatment, I was confronted with a second cancer, lymphoma. I decided I'd better figure out where the dis-ease was in my life and begin developing overall health. My husband, Jerry, speaks of health as being much larger than a healthy body. I needed all-around health: healthy relationships with everyone, including difficult family members, a healthy relationship with myself; and a congruent life. The final revelation came to me when I realized that a core issue of my dis-ease was that I had no relationship to spirit. I knew how to clean up some messy relationships, but I knew nothing about spiritual connection and even after I was on a healthy hike down that road, the entire notion of God was pretty much impossible. I was really much too smart to believe in the existence of a man in the sky…but what about the billions of people who do worship a deity? Was I missing something?

I started this journey seriously (as opposed to just mucking about the subject) about ten years ago. It has been a joyous experience. It has been frustrating and it has not been without some dark nights of the soul. There has been loss. This journey is like learning a new language, one that some people in your life don't speak. Some people can even exhibit a bit of hostility towards it. Once upon a time I did as well. Inevitably when one door opens another closes, and having to let go of long-cherished things and people has been sad. But beyond good fortune, my husband, another east coast intellectual with whom the subject of spiritual belief never came up during our thirty-some years of marriage, found my exploration interesting and has become a great source of comfort and partnership. We've successfully partnered in so many things, but I wasn't sure about this new direction of mine. Nor was he. But he is on board and together we are vibrantly engaged in a much-enhanced life together.

And so ten years after this diagnosis of a life-threatening disease I am completely healthy. My cancer is either gone or quiet; the side effects of the cancers and treatments are gone. New people with similar worldviews are filling our lives with marvelous conversation. I have a new spiritual toolbox to draw from.

This newfound spiritual balance has helped me get through a more recent challenge, when my younger sister became frighteningly ill and died. In the aftermath, I suffered what I call a psychic explosion. It might be called a depression. I could hear our dead mother's critical voice yelling at me every time I was triggered by some insignificant mistake or frustration. I cried, and I blasted myself with rageful invective when I made trivial mistakes. I had no energy and there were days when I could do nothing but watch paint dry. My youngest daughter and I began family therapy which is much more intense than I would have imagined, and the writing of this book loomed as impossibly beyond my ability.

But because of my journey, I knew what to do. I read a little and allowed my mood to dictate my actions. I watched a tremendous amount of Netflix (which I highly recommend). I managed to maintain good habits by exercising regularly, eating well, meditating, setting intentions, and journaling. I had two sessions with the therapist I'm seeing with my daughter, two good massages, one acupuncture session and one session with my homeopathy doctor. Slowly, I began to heal. My sister died on September 30th; and on February 1st I felt I could declare myself back. Last night my husband and I were visiting with our two little dogs. As he left the room he said, "I'm glad you're back! I like this version of you much better."

Having a personal theology is good in the same way that having money is good: it expands your choices and gives you options you do not have in its absence. Once you are plugged in to a spiritual connection, you have choices you didn't know existed. The stronger the spiritual connection, the more the choices. Anyone is capable of plugging in to such a connection, and I'm hoping that this book will be helpful to anyone who wants to. If I had to state one great insight from this exploration of mine, I would have to say that even though it seemed impossible, I was finally able to move from a vision of God as a man in the sky to one that is abstract. I have a sense that a lot of others, dissatisfied with religion and spirituality, might be faced with the same dilemma. I didn't think I'd ever get there, but I did. Hopefully this book will show how I did it.

The development of a personal theology is not a linear journey. This book takes apart the things I have put together to form my own theology. It is a meandering path and I have traveled it from almost no spiritual connection to a robust one which has enriched my life in ways I could never have predicted. Although there are scholarly references, I am hoping that the personal reflections and the example of my own transformation will allow others to look at their own lives and expand their own spiritual connections as well.

I write this not as an expert, but as a seeker.

I think it is important to understand at the beginning that this entire journey was about three things. First, I received the amazing insight that I did not really understand the things I thought I understood. I became insecure about my certainty and I became suspicious of other people's certainty. This state of uncertainty was the beginning of a wonderful exploration, making my discoveries crisp and fresh. Second, I needed to get healthy in the largest sense. And finally, when I was able to sense the divine in myself and the spiritual realm beyond myself, I had to come to terms with the notion of God.

What follows is as good an explication of that journey as I can come up with.

CHAPTER ONE

HOW MYSTERY AND PRECISION LED ME TO WONDER ABOUT GOD

There came a time about ten years ago when I was unsure of just about everything. I kept finding myself confronted with the awareness that I did not understand a lot of things I once thought I understood very well. And my questions were not limited to my own understanding: when others, even experts, expressed strongly worded opinions or even facts, I wondered how they knew that for sure? I gradually came to realize that my understanding was slanted and incomplete. My beliefs were smaller than they needed to be. As we will see beliefs are both intractable and malleable. I came to these beliefs honestly from my culture, my family, my education, my associations and my own personal interests. But as my worldview changed, I began being unsure of what I knew or believed. I will talk more about worldview later on, but for now, here is a story involving changing beliefs.

As a young woman I believed that I could never have enough of what I needed. I was more rooted in scarcity than abundance. In my twenties I moved into an intentional community, and my life was thrown off-balance as I began living mostly communally. When we are off-balance things often come into new focus—and in my off-balance state, many things about myself came into focus. One was that I was less generous than I wished to be. I held on to things after they were no longer useful. For example, I had moved into the community with a chenille double bedspread that I thought was very nice, but I was living in a small room that I shared with another woman. We had twin beds, and I had no room to store the bedspread, so I decided that I should pass it on to someone who could actually use it. The person I chose accepted the bedspread but did not fall down with gratitude as I'd imagined he would. This experience taught me a lot about giving and receiving. I gave the bedspread away because I wanted to be generous. He accepted it. Cycle completed. So why was I still dissatisfied? I came to realize that even if the recipient did not seem to fully appreciate how special the bedspread was, this was not my business. What was really bothering me was that I believed that I would not be able to get another full-size bedspread if I were to need one in the future. *I believed there wasn't enough.*

That core belief did not change at once, but my desire to be a more generous person enabled me to begin the process of trying to change. I wanted to be more generous because I thought generous people were more interesting than less generous people. My desire was to be happy with what I had and not worry about what I did not or could not have. After I married Jerry, who is a very easy-going person, I realized that when I ironed our clothes (which I did infrequently), I always ironed my stuff first because if I got tired of ironing he wouldn't mind having less clothing to choose from. I stopped doing that in the name of becoming a more generous person, and made it a practice to always iron his clothing before mine. It was somewhat uncomfortable, but I was doing it for a purpose—to remind myself that in fact I *did* have enough.

These are what I call little drills. I *believed* that I didn't have enough. I *believed* that I had to hold on to what I had because I might never get it again. This theme of deprivation grew from the way I was raised. But through these little drills I was able to make the changes I needed to make to actually become generous. I changed. I now think about paying back, giving back, doing more much of the time. I think I really did become generous, but the only way I could touch the belief that got in the way of being generous (*I don't have enough*) was to change my worldview. The only way I could change my worldview was by acting differently than what felt natural, and my drills enabled me to do that. The rewards have been significant. I now see myself as having so much more than I need that being generous has become natural and even necessary. I use this as a personal example of how a deeply embedded belief, like *I don't have enough*, can be transformed by a shift in worldview. These little drills are the basis of change for me. They work. As I have evolved they have evolved into practices which I will describe later.

But what if there really *isn't* enough, the skeptic will ask. Mustn't we recognize "reality"? I feel it necessary to clear up the word "reality" before we get too far into the discussion of personal theology. Discussion about theology, spirit, etc. seems to invite pushback: *Can any of this be proven?* I translate this to mean *is this experience of spirit real or is it just in your imagination?* The skeptic states, "you can't prove any of this and until I can see proof I remain an unbeliever, atheist, materialist, scientist, realist, etc." In my experience many people equate reality with the material: if something can be experienced through the five senses, sight, hearing, touch, taste and smell—then it is real. If it is real it can be measured. How does one measure spirit? One doesn't. One experiences spirit. Another way of expressing this pushback is that what is *out there* is real, and what is *in here* (inside us) is not. The placebo effect is a great example of this kind of doubt or pushback. In most double-blind studies testing medications, one group is given the new medication while a control group is given a sugar pill. Most of the time the participants, and even the doctors, do not know to which group they have been assigned. In a large number of cases (often 40 percent or more) the people taking the placebo present signs of healing: their symptoms are reduced and their disease sometimes eliminated. Although not much is known about how the placebo effect works, it is believed that when a person thinks they are getting help, their body goes into a state of well-being which enables the immune system to rise to the task and create the necessary chemicals to heal the body. As Rudolph Ballentine tells us, while "in our culture we see healing as coming from 'outside' ourselves…the placebo effect is telling us that healing comes from 'within.'"[1] The placebo effect points to a kind of super-intelligence that exists in each of us, possessed of technical know-how far beyond our present understanding. According to Patricia Norris, we are a country with the deeply embedded belief that what cannot be measured does not exist. She states that if a piece of information does not fit a theory it is considered *noise* and discarded or at best disregarded. We know that the placebo effect is real and we also know that spontaneous remissions of diseases are real, but since we cannot measure or explain these phenomena we simply ignore them.[2]

An Indian spiritual master once told a devotee, "The physical world is very convincing. It seems solid and reliable. How can you possibly escape it? By seeing that this world is actually a product of your mind. Without that realization, the physical world wraps around you like a net. But all nets have holes. Find one and jump through."[3]

I'm suggesting that when you jump through the holes

[1] Rudolph Ballentine, M.D., *Radical Healing*, (Honesdale: Himalayan Institute, 2011).

[2] Patricia Norris and Barrett Porter, *Why Me? Harnessing the Healing Power of the Human Spirit* (Walpole: Stillpoint Publishing, 1985).

[3] Deepak Chopra, *The Future of God: A Practical Approach to Spirituality for Our Times* (Nevada City: Harmony Books, 2015).

in the net, you are going to find a new angle on reality—
you are going to encounter **mystery**. Mystery, or things not
easily categorized or explained, includes the things that are
near to your heart—the things that really matter to you:
red and blue, bitter and sweet, physical pain and physical
delight, beautiful and ugly, good and bad, God and
eternity. The world of mystery includes meaning and hope,
emotions and aspirations, love and suffering, intuition and
direct knowing.[4] And then there is longing, compassion,
empathy, control, power, humor, joy, grief and loss. Can
they be measured? Why would we want to measure them?
They are mysteriously wonderful, and perhaps they are
wonderful precisely because they are mysterious.

I make the assumption that many people think science
will ultimately prove the existence or non-existence
of God. There is actually a conversation that supposes
quantum physics will provide the ultimate answer to the
question of the existence of God. I quote a few scientists
who contributed to a book called *Quantum Questions*
because they do not see any path to such "proof" and are
able to find no contradiction between science and mystery.
Scientific findings, especially those in physics, have poked
big holes in our understanding of the universe. Many of the
scientists in *Quantum Questions* say that science can only
give symbolic knowledge—it can tell you how something
behaves, but not what something is. If you want to fill those

---

[4] Deepak Chopra, *Reinventing the Body, Resurrecting the Soul* (New
York: Three Rivers Press, 2010).

gaps of understanding with spirituality, these scientists say, go ahead, but use the methods derived from mysticism to do so, not science. The language of mysticism is closer to that of poetry than to the precision-oriented language of natural science. Thus we ought not to intermingle the two languages; we should think more subtly than we have hitherto been accustomed to do. The care to be taken in keeping the two languages, religious and scientific, apart from one another should also include an avoidance of any weakening of their content by blending them. As Einstein put it, "The present fashion of applying the axioms of physical science to human life is not only entirely a mistake but has also something reprehensible in it."[5] If the language of science describes behavior as opposed to reality it leaves the door wide open to whether or not there is a God. My only point here is to go deeper. Science and spirit are not opposed if looked at conceptually.

Not knowing is okay. Mystery moves us toward intuition, which Einstein himself said is "the only real valuable thing." Intuition, he said, "leads us into new territory, allowing us to play with new ideas from which magnificent breakthroughs can develop. If at first an idea is not absurd, then there is no hope for it."[6]

I am going to do my very best to eliminate the word "reality" from this book. I shall refer only to experience.

[5] See Ken Wilber, ed., *Quantum Questions: Mystical Writings of the World's Greatest Physicists* (Boston: Shambhala Publications, 2000).

[6] Geral Blanchard, *Ancient Ways: Indigenous Healing Innovations for the 21st Century* (Holyoke: Neari Press, 2011), 83.

Another assumption of this book is that embracing the mysteries in our lives is as rewarding and fulfilling as embracing what we agree upon as being "real". And we certainly do not have to all embrace mystery in the same way.

It would seem at first glance that precision is the absolute opposite of mystery. At least it seemed to me that they were incompatible. And yet the notion of precision called to me and somehow seemed juxtaposed to mystery. Poised against the mystery of spirit is the **precision** of the natural world. While mystery is big, broad, expansive and almost wild, precision is tight, clean, exact, and orderly. They seem almost opposite. I am comfortable with mystery because I now realize that mystery shrouds much that is meaningful in our lives. But in a way the precision of the universe evokes more thorny questions. The slightest shift in the orbit of a planet could cause them to crash into one another, and yet this never happens. Every maple tree has leaves of an exact, easily recognizable shape. Our bodies tick along with trillions of chemical reactions going on every second. Our world operates according to clear, predictable laws, like the law of gravity. We all understand this law and follow it, or else. We will fall off that wobbly ladder if we don't take note of gravity.

But if there are laws are there lawmakers? In speaking of precision we inevitably come to the question of creation. Deepak Chopra talks about precision and creation in terms that recall Einstein's claim that there is a central order to the cosmos that can be directly apprehended by the soul in mystical union. Chopra writes:

The real issue—and this is where the controversy starts—is whether creation came out of "nothing," that is a nonphysical source. Is there room in that nothingness for higher organization, the kind of mind that could have perfectly fit the laws of nature together to such a finely tuned degree that the slightest change would have spelled doom for the early universe? After all, with an alteration of less than a billionth in the law of gravity, for example, the nascent universe would have collapsed in on itself after the Big Bang: an alteration in the opposite direction would have caused it to fly apart in uncontrollable winds of proto-gasses, never to form atoms and molecules. The fine-tuning of the universe is indisputable, and we are the direct beneficiaries. Somehow creation emerged in such perfect harmony that human DNA arrived on the scene thirteen billion years later.[7]

The following passage is my absolute favorite and expresses what I see as true regarding the belief that we live in a random universe.

In 1982 the British astrophysicist Sir Fred Hoyle gave a radio lecture in which he mentioned in passing that, "a colleague of mine worked out that a yeast cell and a 747 airplane had the same number of parts, the same level of complexity." The current scientific explanation for how all the complex parts of a yeast cell came together is

---

[7] Chopra, *The Future of God.*

randomness. Hoyle tried to calculate how unlikely it was that random chance has assembled a living cell. The odds were very low. But what has survived is a striking analogy that doesn't depend upon whether he got his numbers right (the model of airplane changed along the way): the chance that higher life forms might have emerged in this way [i.e. randomly] is comparable to the chance that a tornado sweeping through a junkyard might assemble a Boeing 747 from materials therein.[8]

I am abandoning the notion of randomness as a factor in my theology because it simply makes no sense to me. There may be a place for it, but I haven't quite come up with an understanding of how randomness and law can go hand in hand. It is a better fit for me to believe that there is purpose, meaning and precision to our lives. (Another reader might find randomness interesting and would probably develop a theology that looks different from mine, which is why I so believe in the development of personal theology.)

So we have these two notions: mystery and precision. Mystery leaves us with the idea that certain things cannot be easily explained. But precision, which one would think would eliminate the mystery of understanding, seems to lead us to the same conclusion simply because the precision we have discussed is itself mysterious. If we humans as a species are imbued with a need for meaning—and I certainly have that need—then we need to look for meaning or explanation. If we eliminate randomness as an

---

[8] Chopra, *The Future of God*, 49.

option, both mystery and precision point in the direction of a god—a lawmaker, force, energy, field, source—behind the creation of all that is. So let's begin to take that on.

CHAPTER TWO

Is It Possible To Transform "The Man In The Sky" Into Something Bigger?

As I stated before, my spiritual journey began late in life. I began to suspect that everything I thought I knew was uncertain when I was 54. In 1996, I had breast cancer, for which I was treated with a lumpectomy and radiation. I had little discomfort other than mild lymphedema, which is the swelling of the arm, and periodic systemic infections, which are sometimes a side effect of the treatment. I paid attention to these symptoms, but I did not make significant changes to my life. Eight years later, during a routine exam, my doctor discovered an enlarged spleen and that led to a diagnosis of lymphoma. By this time I had known my doctor, Dr. Joel Bernstein, for eight years and truly loved him. Because of my trust in this brilliant and generous man, I went home after my diagnosis, sat quietly in a comfortable chair in my bedroom and said to myself: *You are going to hand this cancer over to Dr. B—and you are going to sit in this chair and figure out how to get healthy. You are going to figure out where the dis-ease is in your life.* Five months later I walked back into my life with the answer: I had to develop a connection to spirit if I was going to become healthy.

By the time I got to graduate school, after about a year of intense spiritual study on my own, it was impossible to ignore the dreaded word. God! God and religion have a primary seat at the table of spirituality and both were concepts I was uncomfortable with. Just how was I going to come to terms with the idea of a man in the sky monitoring billions of people's lives as well as holding gravity steady? This was not going to be easy—and in fact it wasn't!

I grew up in working-class Brooklyn and I was Jewish in name only. It was a widely held belief in my Jewish family and community that being Jewish was a really good thing, but there was not much to substantiate that belief other than some great food. Yet in spite of the fact that there was no God in my household, I somehow knew all about that man in the sky. My image of God was clear: he was seated on a throne in a blast of white—white throne, white robes, white hair, white skin, white flowing beard, all supported by white billowing clouds. This image is stronger within me than the image of my father pushing me on the swings when I was three, shortly before he died. And to confuse matters entirely, after my father died I knew that he was up there watching out for me as well. He could see me and the wonder of me when everyone else seemed to see me as a problem.

So in my developing brain there was confusion—confusion I must say still persists. Even though I could not intellectually accept the notion of a man in the sky, every single time I heard the word God, there he was.

As a young college student I easily made the decision to pursue a life devoid of religion or spirit; I chose to identify with people who in the name of greater intellect denied the existence of a higher being of any kind. Upon deeper reflection I think I was rejecting the notion of a God in the sky who basically granted or denied wishes—but as Karen Armstrong says, the denial of God (or atheism) should be looked upon as a starting point for examining a religion or belief system that is no longer working or relevant.[1]

I managed to simply ignore the subject of spirit for the better part of my adulthood. My life looked a bit like Deepak Chopra's description in his book, *The Future of God.* He basically says that if you take a hundred babies and film their entire lives it would not be possible to identify those who believe in God or predict that they would be happier, wiser, or more successful than the non-believers. Someone who has experienced God may look upon the world with wonder and joy, but the video camera cannot record what is happening below the surface. I looked like just about anyone else, but had far less inner life than outer. I would say that my emotions and experiences before my spiritual conversion were more blunted.

---

[1] Karen Armstrong, *A History of God: The 4000-Year Quest of Judaism, Christianity and Islam* (New York: Ballentine, 1993).

The idea of an anthropomorphic God makes perfect sense when looked at developmentally and historically. Historically speaking I am a thoroughly Western educated person and I live in a material world. In his book *Radical Healing*, Rudolph Ballentine talks about our culture as being both materialistic and reductive. We recognize only that which we can know through our senses. If we cannot see it, hear it, smell it, touch it or taste it—it simply does not exist. So, when we come up with a phenomenon that cannot be explained materially (such as the placebo effect), we discard that information or say that it is irrelevant. As an extension of this paradigm we tend to reduce things to their smallest parts instead of seeing things as part of systems. If our knee hurts, we find the part or parts of that knee that are causing the problem and treat them with drugs or surgery. An Eastern way of knowing, however, would approach that knee with much more mystery as well as a more holistic approach. The knee issue might be treated in a multitude of ways such as manipulation, diet, herbs, acupuncture, homeopathy, exercise, etc. Our material way of thinking permeates our culture and shapes the way we think about things, including God. But as I will show our way of thinking is not set in stone: there are levels of knowing or evolutions of thought and we can move through these levels. If we move through these levels, our beliefs and worldviews can evolve or grow.

Level 1 (Fight-or-Flight Response)	You fulfill your life through family, community, a sense of belonging and material comforts. Your identity is based upon your physical body and physical environment.
Level 2 (Reactive Response)	You fulfill your life through success, power, influence, status, and other ego satisfactions. Your identity is based on ego and personality.
Level 3 (Restful Awareness Response)	You fulfill your life through peace, centeredness, self-acceptance, and inner silence. Your identity is based upon silent witness.
Level 4 (Intuitive Response)	You fulfill your life through insight, empathy, tolerance, and forgiveness. Your identity is based upon the knower within.
Level 5 (Creative Response)	You fulfill your life through inspiration, expanded creativity in art or science, and unlimited discovery. Your identity is based upon being a co-creator with God.
Level 6 (Visionary Response)	You fulfill your life through reverence, compassion, devoted service, and universal love. Your identity is based upon enlightenment.
Level 7 (Sacred Response)	You fulfill your life through wholeness and unity with the divine. Your identity is based upon the source of it all.

In *How to Know God*, Chopra follows this line of development and sees our relation to God and the development of that relationship in evolutionary terms. Relationships evolve all the time. My relationship with my husband has evolved over thirty-six years; we've figured out so many things and relate differently than we did thirty, twenty or even ten years ago. We laugh a lot more and our discussions have much greater depth than they did when we were younger. One's relationship with God can evolve in much the same way.

Chopra compares the levels of knowing God to biological processes. Those familiar with the energetic system of Chakras will see that these levels roughly equate with the ascending levels of our chakras. In short, "If you accept that the world is as we are, it is only logical to accept that God is as we are."[2]

Chopra describes a God that matches each of the seven levels outlined above.

[2] Deepak Chopra, *How to Know God* (New York: Three Rivers Press, 2001), 49.

Level 1 (Fight-or-Flight Response)	You fulfill your life through family, community, a sense of belonging and material comforts. Your identity is based upon your physical body and physical environment.	God the protector fits a world of bare survival, full of physical threats and danger.
Level 2 (Reactive Response)	You fulfill your life through success, power, influence, status, and other ego satisfactions. Your identity is based on ego and personality.	God the almighty fits a world of power struggles and ambition, where fierce competition rules.
Level 3 (Restful Awareness Response)	You fulfill your life through peace, centeredness, self-acceptance, and inner silence. Your identity is based upon silent witness.	A God of peace fits a world of inner solitude where reflection and contemplation are possible.
Level 4 (Intuitive Response)	You fulfill your life through insight, empathy, tolerance, and forgiveness. Your identity is based upon the knower within.	God the redeemer fits a world where personal growth is encouraged and insights prove fruitful.
Level 5 (Creative Response)	You fulfill your life through inspiration, expanded creativity in art or science, and unlimited discovery. Your identity is based upon being a co-creator with God.	God the creator fits a world that is constantly renewing itself where innovation and discovery are valued.
Level 6 (Visionary Response)	You fulfill your life through reverence, compassion, devoted service, and universal love. Your identity is based upon enlightenment.	A God of miracles fits a world that contains prophets and seers, where spiritual vision is nurtured.
Level 7 (Sacred Response)	You fulfill your life through wholeness and unity with the divine. Your identity is based upon the source of it all.	A God of pure being— "I Am"—fits a world that transcends all boundaries, a world of infinite possibilities.

So at the first level of *flight or fight response:* you fulfill your life through family, community, a sense of belonging and material comforts. Your identity is based upon your physical body and physical environment. And the God appropriate for this level would be *God the Protector.* Based upon both the paradigm of materialism and reduction and this first developmental level it makes perfect sense that an early relationship with God would be a man in the sky—a mix of Superman and Santa Claus.

That pretty much lines up with my earliest ideas of God, and it does for a lot of people. Karen Armstrong states, "My ideas about God were formed in childhood and did not keep abreast of my growing knowledge in other disciplines."[3] The problem is that as we mature into adulthood and through adulthood, this representation of God might be inadequate to our adult selves.

Luckily, we don't need to be stuck there forever. At the critical time that I made the decision to become healthy I experienced God in a different way. My decision to restrict the activities of my life while I concentrated on figuring out how to be healthy was inspired, and it filled me with wonder. It was a bold and uncharacteristic move on my part, if only because it meant taking a lot of "off" time and saying no to many activities. I knew that the inspiration for that decision didn't come solely from within. I can't tell you how I knew what to do. I just did. It was my first brush with intuition and it felt different from the way in

---

[3] Armstrong, *A History of God*, xix.

which I usually obtained information. And yet there was no doubt. I knew exactly what I had to do and I sat and I listened and I read and I made lists. And once I had formed that intention to get well and made the space for it, information and connections came pouring in. I met Carolyn Myss through a friend. Norm Shealy came to me through Carolyn Myss and I found Holos University through Norm Shealy. That is how it works. Intention and intuition are spiritual. I shall connect the dots as we move along.

For now we will leave God right here at this early stage of development.

CHAPTER THREE

SPIRITUAL BUT NOT RELIGIOUS

I like to connect dots. Through all of my life's many transformations and evolutions, each time I arrive at a new place I like to look back and find the thread that I began pulling upon that has brought me to my present paradigm.

When I look back at my spiritual growth, that thread connects back to the point when I began to suspect that what I thought was true might not be. At first this was disconcerting. Not only did I distrust my own information, but I doubted others. When a friend emphatically denigrated a public figure I wondered why she felt so strongly—after all, she didn't even know the person. How did she know her information was correct or complete? I became a constant, equal-opportunity doubter. In defense of myself, I think I was on the right track. Gregg Braden estimates that we humans only have information concerning about 2 percent of what is available to us.[1] That means 98 percent of the

---

[1] Gregg Braden, *The Spontaneous Healing of Belief: Shattering the Paradigm of False Limits* (Carlsbad: Hay House, 2009).

information contained within the multiverse is unknown to us. Even if this statistic is grossly exaggerated, it tells us a lot about ourselves. We don't know that much and what we do know will most probably be impacted by future information.

After my second cancer diagnosis, I sat in my bedroom for about five months, and the great realization hit me: I had no conscious spiritual connection. I was less openhearted than I wanted to be. I had no connection to soul or spirit and didn't really understand what those words even meant. How was I going to open this connection to spirit, make it more present, and utilize it more abundantly—when at the same time I saw religion as divisive and I knew that divisiveness was not going to be my path? This was my challenge.

As I descended into this place of doubt one question kept nagging at me: Since I was too smart to believe in God, did that imply that everyone who did believe was less smart? I guessed it did. But then who was I to make this judgment? Perhaps there was more to it than had met my eye. There were certainly many intelligent people out there who *did* seem to believe.

The exact statistics vary depending on the poll, but they are overwhelmingly consistent: most people are either religious or believe in God, and at the same time there is a trend toward people declaring themselves as spiritual and not religious. 96 percent of Americans currently profess a belief in God. 42 percent attend religious services regularly.

67 percent consider their RS (Religious and Spiritual) beliefs as very important in their lives. 47 percent associate frequent religious involvement with greater happiness.[2] Gregg Braden cites a worldwide census of religion from 2000, which "is believed to be the most accurate accounting of our world in recorded history. Among the compelling statistics that the survey revealed about our global family, and perhaps the most telling, is our nearly universal sense that we're here on purpose, and we're not alone. Over 95% of the world's population believes in the existence of a higher power. Of that number, over half call that power 'God'."[3]

Regardless of the exact numbers, the fact seems to be that the vast majority of people find meaning and answers through their connection to God, religion, and spirituality. But one thing about these statistics is changing.

In their book *Living Deeply: The Art and Science of Transformation in Everyday Life,* Marilyn Schlitz, Cassandra Vieten, and Tina Amorok describe a groundswell of people who have "become disillusioned with organized religion and seek alternative forms of spiritual practice to provide meaning and purpose." The "spiritual," they have found, outweighs the "religious":

Our survey sample reflects this movement: although 60 percent were raised in a religious household and 40

---

[2] Carl E. Thoresen and Alex H.S. Harris, "Spirituality and Health: What's the Evidence and What's Needed?" *Annals of Behavioral Medicine* 24, no. 1 (2002).

[3] Braden, *The Spontaneous Healing of Belief,* 5.

percent were not, only 30 percent identified themselves as religious without another spiritual practice, while 70 percent identified themselves as spiritual, not religious. Moreover, a full 95 percent reported that they were very or moderately spiritual, whereas only 22 percent considered themselves very or moderately religious.[4]

This move from people declaring themselves religious toward declaring themselves as spiritual is growing. Even though many people equate the two, it is helpful to think of "spiritual" and "religious" as different things. Certainly, many religious people are spiritual, but many are not; they like the ritual, tradition, and ceremony and do not necessarily experience much of a spiritual connection in their faith. Religion may be a social configuration, a habit, an unquestioned part of their life.

This is not to say that people cannot find spiritual connection through religion. My point is that a person can have a fully spiritual life in the absence of religion. If you are born into or find a religion that meets your needs, you are lucky. I tried that. I tried a bit of Judaism, Buddhism, and Zen meditation, and I attended services at the Self Realization center here in Encinitas, California. They all gave me something, but not what I needed. My aim was to strengthen my spiritual connection, but a ready-made doctrine did not work for me. I had to find my own way.

---

[4] Marilyn Schlitz, Cassandra Vieten, and Tina Amorok, *Living Deeply: The Art and Science of Transformation in Everyday Life*, (Oakland: New Harbinger Publications, 2008), 90.

In the end, I would say I am "spiritual" without being "religious." I find the study of all religion fascinating, and I find that any house of worship fills my spirit and soul with energy. The community of worshipers enlarges the experience of spiritual energy. But I am not religiously affiliated. Many religions seem more divisive and dualistic than I am comfortable with; as in my religion is better than yours or my God is better than yours. Holism is my religion.

At this juncture we will begin looking at what might be driving this shift in people's self-image from identifying as religious to identifying as spiritual and how thought, belief, and consciousness might be coming into play. Since thought, belief, and consciousness are inner activities I want to take a look at the development of inner life.

CHAPTER FOUR

SPIRITUALITY REQUIRES BALANCING THE INNER AND OUTER

We all balance many elements in our lives. On a daily basis we negotiate family, friends, work, play, religion, and the issues that we feel passionate about. In my case I am a wife, mother, grandmother, friend, business owner, writer, knitter, reader, student, and spiritual seeker. When I was diagnosed with my second cancer, my question was, where is the *dis-ease* in my life? A close look at my material life showed me that some of the dis-ease was in my close relationships that were in need of repair. Shortly after I set the intention to repair them, two friendships faded away. I also worked to establish and maintain better boundaries with my aunt, although as a result our relationship was strained until she died several years later. And I gradually resolved the relationship with the greatest dis-ease—the one with my sister—in a positive way, giving us seven good years together before she died. I consider these "outer adjustments" or adjustments to my material life. By releasing toxic and drama-laden relationships I certainly felt healthier and believe I became healthier.

I felt strongly that this process of attaining better health I'd placed myself in was divinely inspired. I could not, and still cannot, fathom that I was smart enough, wise enough, centered enough, intelligent enough, or holistic enough to figure out on my own that my answer to good health was within me. The more I read about healing as opposed to treatment and cure, the more I realized that healing required a spiritual connection and I had none. I came to understand that without this connection I could not find the balance I was after—and so the burning question of my life became, how do I consciously establish this connection? If divinity powered this transformative place I now found myself in, I wanted more of it. I wanted to strengthen that connection so that I could use it throughout my life, not just for healing my body. By cleaning up my "outer world" I became ready and able to give my inner world serious attention. The balance that was needed was between my inner and outer lives.

I lived in an outer world that consisted of all the roles and institutions I was involved in, and that outer world demanded constant evaluation and re-evaluation to keep it balanced. As I pursued this line of inquiry, I realized that my inner world demanded no less. At the time, my inner world consisted of my brain and body; I lived mostly between my ears, and in my body when it ached. Words started coming to my inner world through my readings and once again I was faced with the understanding that

I had no clue as to what these words meant and how they related to one another. Brain, mind, heart, personality, ego, soul, and spirit are words we are all familiar with, but what exactly do they mean? And how are they related to one another?

If I was going to become healthy, I needed to pay as much attention to my inner world as to my outer world. I needed to find "spiritual homeostasis." So perhaps I needed to start by figuring out the soul. I asked the only practicing Catholic I felt comfortable with to tell me what her definition of soul was. She was unable to provide one, which was my first realization that religious practice and spirituality were not necessarily related. That unanswered question led to years of exploration, as I struggled to get comfortable with these terms and concepts and to manipulate and balance them. On my way to figuring out what I now call soul, I also found a host of other components of the inner world, including heart, ego, personality, and brain. This has added a lot of new elements to my juggling act, but in a way it has made it all easier.

Now when I am faced with a personal or spiritual challenge I not only look at its outer elements, but I also check internally—with heart, ego, brain, and soul. These are complicated concepts; entire tomes have been written dissecting each of the words I am trying to understand and use pragmatically. What follows is a kind of "starter kit" that gives some basic ideas about each.

Heart

We start with the heart, which is a fairly common word in most peoples' vocabularies. How often have we heard someone say *my head says no, but my heart says yes?* We all know what that means. The brain reasoned one way and the heart called to us in another, not necessarily complementary direction. But there is a further implication—a knowing that is subtle and not necessarily conscious. Do we believe the heart can *think* for us? How can the heart say anything? How can the heart, a muscle that pumps blood, tell us what to do?

But in fact, science has shown that our heart does more than beat and pump. It has been described as a "triune" organ that functions on several levels: electromagnetic, neural, and hormonal. According to writer Joseph Chilton Pearce, the heart contains within it its own "brain" that communicates with the cranial brain by means of hormones—which implies that the heart actually does affect emotion.[1] William Tiller puts it this way:

Some higher band qualities of the heart are love, care, appreciation, forgiveness, humor, compassion, patience, tolerance and kindness. Love, in this context, is defined as benevolent heart focus towards the well-being of others and it is found that the heart-focused feeling for any of these mentioned qualities produces profound electrophysiological changes in heart rate and variability

---

[1] Joseph Chilton Pearce, *The Biology of Transcendence: A Blueprint of the Human Spirit* (Rochester: Park Street Press, 2002).

(HRV) as contrasted with the mental focus on the concept of these heart qualities, which does not produce such HRV changes.[2]

This may sound confusing, but it is simply the difference between thinking about love and actually feeling love. I access this heartfelt love by giving my heart attention and listening to what it has to say. I find that I make more and more decisions that come from my heart as opposed to my head.

The electromagnetic energy that emanates from the heart forms an arc that folds back on itself; this is a very stable form for energy, which once generated and set in motion, tends to self perpetuate.

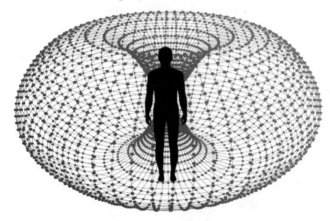

[Adapted from Joseph Chilton Pearce, *The Biology of Transcendence: A Blueprint of the Human Spirit* (Rochester: Park Street Press, 2002).]

---

[2] William A. Tiller, *Science and Human Transformation: Subtle Energies, Intentionality and Consciousness* (Walnut Creek: Pavior Publishing, 1997), 213.

The diagram above is how I interpret and generalize heart energy. This large extension of electromagnetic energy radiates approximately 12 to 14 feet all around each of us. This energy arcs out from and curves back to the heart to form a torus, or field. This energy flows up through our chakras and also down through our chakras on an axis or dipole of the heart torus. This form extends far beyond the human individual. The sun's energy also has this torus quality, and apparently the very solar system does as well. All of our energies are interacting.

This simply illustrates that the heart is more than we generally think, although as I've said on some level we all know this. We know when something is heartfelt and when something is heartless. I often think of my torus and wonder if the people that I chafe at don't have a lot of static in theirs. Sometimes when my torus mixes with theirs I intuit that they are not living from their hearts.

Ego and Personality

Ego and personality also figure into this "spiritual homeostasis" by which I mean inner and outer life being in balance. Ego and personality are not often thought of as inner qualities, but I believe they weigh in just as heavily as soul and spirit do. If ego and personality become too dominant, other inner qualities can be depressed so understanding them is the first step in controlling them.

In his book *A New Earth,* Eckhart Tolle talks at length about the ego, which he says is basically our false self. It is the part of us that craves recognition and affirmation and it is also the part of us that longs for the status quo. If we find we need constant attention and approval, our egos might possibly be out of balance. Tolle says that recognizing your ego is the first step to putting it in its proper place. I have learned to do that. I can actually tell when mine is waving to me from the corner of my eye and I can then decide if I want it to go away or I want to feed it. My choice.

When my sister died I gave a eulogy at her memorial service. The gathering laughed and cried and they learned things only a sister could tell them. I felt pretty terrific about my performance. And at the same time I wondered how much of what I was feeling was ego? A small part was. I delivered it well. I felt accomplished. I got approval. But on a deeper level I spoke from my heart with great love for the sister with whom I had struggled practically all our lives.

Personality is fixed. One person is timid, another bold, another quiet, another dramatic and loud. When someone says *take it or leave it that's just the way I am,* they are talking about personality. Having cared for many babies, I can tell you in no uncertain terms, that they all have distinct personalities practically out of the womb. However, while personality is fixed, we can alter how we *express* our personalities to some limited extent. Very noisy people, people who must be heard, are probably not going to become quiet, only less noisy—but they can learn to listen better and hold back a bit. I used to joke that my husband had Valium running through his veins because he never seemed to get angry—in fact I worried that this might be a bit unhealthy. He listened and has begun to express anger when he is miffed at me—but it can be hard not to laugh when he does because the expression of anger is so alien to his personality that he actually sounds like someone pretending to be angry.

Brain and Mind

The difference between brain and mind is at the heart of current controversy. I conclude from my readings that we are in the midst of a great paradigm shift here. Some scientists (but not all) still hold fast to the idea that the mind is part of the brain, which is all-powerful and controls other elements of our being such as mind, ego, soul, etc. The new paradigm, though, says that mind is much more than the collection of neurons and synapses that make up our brains. I reject the traditional scientific view, and although I am far from a deep understanding I've sorted it out this way.

The way I see it, the brain is like my hard drive. It is responsible for the control of autonomous body functions and controls much of what I think of as my hard-wiring. I have a poor sense of direction. I have learned how to manage that by compensating with all kinds of props, but basically my brain just does not seem to map well regarding directionality. The mind, on the other hand, is the part of me that chews up and digests information, some of which comes from my brain and some of which comes from my body, spirit, etc. This distinction in and of itself deserves an entire book, but the following resources can give the reader an idea of how I came to my (admittedly rudimentary) understanding.

Sufi teacher Hazrat Inayat Khan said that thought "cannot be limited and restricted to the brain, although the brain is the medium by which thoughts are made clear," adding that "Mind works through the brain and uses the brain."[3] According to Khan's Sufi beliefs, mind and heart are inextricably related: "Mind is the surface of the heart, and the heart is the depth of the mind. Therefore, mind and heart are two names of the one thing. If you call it mind, then its depth is heart; if you call it heart than [sic] its surface is mind."[4] Nothing escapes the purview of the mind, according to Khan; it is the seat of imagination and thought and it reaches into morality, fate, memory, destiny and will.

What the mind needs is stillness. Khan often likened mind to water: when the surface of water is still, reflections are clearly seen, but when the surface is ruffled, everything becomes unclear. Our minds get little rest—even when the body sleeps, the mind is actively involved in dreaming—so we must provide rest for the mind. Later in the book we will talk about ways to gain stillness, but this is as good a

---

[3] Hazrat Inayat Khan, *Spiritual Dimensions of Psychology* (New Lebanon: Omega Publications, 2012), 27.
[4] Khan, *Spiritual Dimensions of Psychology*, 27.

place as any to suggest that meditation is probably one of the greatest gifts we can give to our active minds.

A small but growing number of scientists also have embraced the idea that the mind is not just a matter of the brain. Candace Pert's work places memory in the body in the form of emotional receptor centers and neuropeptides that link mind and body as one entity. This is complicated science, but its application leads to the understanding that there is no longer a strong distinction to be made between the brain, the mind, and the body.[5]

Similarly, Dr. Bruce Greyson, a psychiatrist at the University of Virginia who has studied near-death experiences for thirty years, has noticed phenomena that sometimes happen to people shortly before they die. As their brains shut down, they often enjoy reprieves from their illness. People suffering from dementia become lucid. Alzheimer's disease patients who have not recognized family members for years suddenly do so. Schizophrenics become clearheaded. If mind returns as the brain shuts down, what does this mean? When an Alzheimer's patient became lucid in those hours or days before death, did their brain spontaneously mend? Where did their restored knowing come from? Does the mind become free to function more comprehensively during this shutting down of the brain? And can the mind explore realms that are not physical, but

---

[5] Candace B. Pert, *Everything You Need to Know to Feel Go(o)d* (Carlsbad: Hay House, 2007).

spiritual?[6]

I've seen this personally as well. About three weeks before my 93-year-old mother died, her legs, which had been so swollen they actually wept and did not fit into any normal leg wear, became completely normal. When my sister was dying and her entire body was shutting down before my eyes, her swollen body too became completely normal. Because of having read about Dr. Greyson's work, I did not take these as good signs. In a way I was prepared for their deaths by what appeared to be spontaneous healing. My mother's and sister's healing may seem to be an example of the body rejuvenating as it is preparing to die, but I'm not certain there isn't some amount of brain/ mind function here as well.

Although I have a working relationship with my mind and brain as separate and yet connected I'm certain there is much more information regarding the brain/mind relationship that is being discovered as I am writing this. Just as we are learning the revolutionary possibility that memory does not reside wholly in the brain, these new insights into the mind-brain relationship are going to reveal important information.

Soul and Spirit

And now to the heart of divinity: soul and spirit. Tilden

---

[6] See Charles Q. Choi, "Peace of Mind! Near-Death Experiences Now Found to Have Scientific Explanations," *Scientific American*, September 12, 2011, https://www.scientificamerican.com/article/ peace-of-mind-near-death/.

Edwards says that even though words like soul and spirit are fuzzy, they strike a deep resonance in many people, as though our hearts know what the words mean, even if our minds can't fully grasp it.[7] I can't say that I feel settled in the sorting of these two parts of myself, but I have come a long way in my understanding. Now, although I still have not come up with a true working definition I do see them as distinct parts of myself with actual outlines. I know, for example, from Edward Tick, Ph.D., who wrote a book called *War and the Soul,* that the soul needs feeding, with good food, beauty, art, music, and love, among other things. When such things are removed from our lives (as happens in war), our souls are damaged. I am going to tell you what those with much more expertise than I have to say about soul and spirit, and then I'll explain how I interpret them in my own life.

Tick defines the soul as "the drive to create and preserve life—that of our own, other people, our community, and the planet—as we participate in the endless creativity of the universe.[8] In *Spiritual Director, Spiritual Companion,* Tilden Edwards says that "*Soul* is the word being used to carry a sense of our large transcendent being."[9] He speaks of the soul as something that helps bridge the gap between the divine and the human and speaks of the divine and

---

[7] Tilden Edwards, *Spiritual Director, Spiritual Companion: Guide to Tending the Soul* (New York: Paulist Press, 2001), 31.

[8] Edward Tick, *War and the Soul: Healing Our Nation's Veterans from Post-Traumatic Stress Disorder* (Wheaton: Quest Books, 2005).

[9] Edwards, *Spiritual Director, Spiritual Companion,* 23.

human dwelling mysteriously together in the center of our being all the time. In *Care of the Soul,* Thomas Moore cautions that "if the soul is neglected it just doesn't go away, it appears symptomatically in obsessions, addictions, violence, and loss of meaning."[10]

In his book *Integral Psychology* Ken Wilber unpacks the links between the soul and psychology: he points out that the word psychology means the study of the psyche, and the word psyche means mind or soul. In the Microsoft Thesaurus, for psyche we find: "self: atman, soul, spirit; subjectivity: higher self, spiritual self, spirit." One is reminded, yet again, that the roots of psychology lie deep within the human soul and spirit. But as Tilden Edwards reminds us, the science of psychology cannot explain the soul. The psyche cannot own the soul. "It does not belong to us. It belongs to God. Soul is not a self-contained box that we can possess. It is an orienting placeless place in our being where our spirit and God's Spirit live as almost-one."[11]

In *The Seat of the Soul,* Gary Zukav tells us that spirituality deals with the world beyond the five senses. It deals with experiences we know to be true but cannot easily explain. Spirituality is about intuition sparked with reverence and an understanding of the sacred essence of each thing, and person, plant, bird and animal. "It is

---

[10] Thomas Moore, *Care of the Soul: A Guide for Cultivating Depth and Sacredness in Everyday Life* (New York: Harper, 1995), xi.

[11] Edwards, *Spiritual Director, Spiritual Companion,* 35.

contact with the interior of beingness."[12] But we often lose touch with these intuitive experiences because we can't explain them. As many scientists have told us, our infatuation with technology and science may have dwarfed conversation about spirit and this imbalance may not be good for humanity.

I am going to conclude my survey of some of what I gleaned from my readings about the soul with a quote from Edward Tick regarding war and trauma. I find that sometimes the study of dysfunction leads us to greater understandings of what functioning means. Tick's book is largely about the damage of war to soldiers in the form of Post-Traumatic Stress Disorder and he speaks of the soul's separation from the body and the effects of that.

In the presence of life-threatening violence, the soul— the true self—flees. The center of experience shifts: the body takes the impact of the trauma but does not register it as deeply as before. With body and soul separated, a person is trapped in a limbo where past and present intermingle without differentiation or continuity. Nothing is right until body and soul rejoin.[13]

In no way am I comparing myself to a veteran with PTSD, but I have to say that in my case, although my soul was quite intact, my lack of conscious connection to it caused me dis-ease in the form of bodily illness. Having

---

[12] Gary Zukav, *The Seat of the Soul: A Remarkable Treatment of Thought, Evolution, and Reincarnation* (New York: Simon & Schuster, 1989), 34.

[13] Tick, *War and the Soul*, 16.

formed that connection, though, I have become healthier than I have ever been.

My spiritual connection does not just make me feel better; it has actually improved my life and those closest to me tremendously, so as a pragmatist I strongly recommend it. My husband, secular to the bone, was a bit upended when I began this journey in earnest. To my wonderment, he has become a full partner on this particular road, because as he watched me emerge from a smaller space to a larger, lighter one, he wanted some of that energy too. I have so many people close to me who wander around in a morass of confusion, seeing no resolution to problems that not only make them unhappy, but also limit their potential. Deepak Chopra also sees a pragmatic element to spirituality. Without it, the messiness of life seems to act like a clog in the decision-making process. We have all experienced patterns of behavior that, try as we might, we cannot seem to unravel and overcome. Chopra's liberating point is that the answers we need to solve complex problems do not lie at the level of the problem. Life's problems make you more aware of your inner purpose, and their answers lie in the realm of spirit, in expanded awareness. He does not believe that crises are random.[14] My doctor treated my cancer, but the answer to my dis-ease was found in spirit—by looking inward and upward I was able to heal and become truly healthy.

---

[14] See Deepak Chopra, *Spiritual Solutions: Answers to Life's Greatest Challenges* (New York: Harmony Books, 2012).

That health extends beyond my own personal well-being. In an essay in the book *Quantum Questions*, Erwin Schrödinger (1887–1961) quotes Aziz Nasafi, a thirteenth century Islamic-Persian mystic.

On the death of any living creature the spirit returns to the spiritual world, the body to the bodily world. In this however only the bodies are subject to change. The spiritual world is one single spirit who stands unto a light behind the bodily world and who, when any single creature comes into being, shines through it as through a window. According to the kind and size of the window less or more light enters the world. The light itself however remains unchanged.[15]

I can say without doubt that in my experience, as I spend more and more time connecting with spirit and soul, my light gets brighter and I add more of it to the world. I'm guessing that this light, which exists to some extent in all of us, shines through a "window" and this window grows larger as we find balance in all of these elements of ourselves and begin to discover spiritual laws.

I love this notion of spiritual laws. Just as the law of gravity guides us to making good decisions on when and when not to climb a ladder, or stand on the counter, etc. spiritual laws guide us in much the same way. Spiritual laws balance material laws. In Dan Millman's little book *The Laws of Spirit,* he takes us on a mountain hike with a traveler sage who teaches spiritual law through contact

---

[15] Wilber, *Quantum Questions*, 87.

with the natural world. We encounter the law of balance, choices, process, presence, compassion faith, expectation, integrity, action, cycles, surrender and finally the Law of Unity.

I may not have a thorough understanding of spirit, but I can tell you that knowledge of these laws has helped me make decisions, and when I follow these laws things tend to work out well. I tend to be a rule follower and I respect authority—for me, it helps to be conscious that there are spiritual laws and that following them not only engenders a sense of well-being, but might even have an effect on human suffering. I do not think of this in terms of ethics and morality, and I reject any assumptions that God, or Field or Source controls human behavior. I believe we control our behavior according to the law of free will. We have the choice of how to act. But that does not mean that spiritual guidelines and laws aren't necessary for *good living*—a way of being that does less harm and causes less suffering to oneself and others.

Even in my secular early life, I have always followed spiritual laws, often unconsciously. To take a possibly simplistic example: We have a friend who only picks up his dog's poop when there are people around. (He actually admits that!) I would never do that. Never! I always pick up poop and on the unusual occasion that I forget a bag, I return to the crime scene and pick it up later. Once upon a time, I would have described my behavior as rigid. But now I see that I was unconsciously acting on the principle that you do the right thing even when it is inconvenient and there are consequences if you don't. I think I have always intuited spiritual law and am grateful for that. But knowing these laws makes it far easier to be and do good.

So, in conclusion to this conversation about soul and spirit I find my soul to be the center of my being, needing daily contact with all that is good and pure and inspiring. My soul is divine. The more it is fed the more I feel it. Spirit is all-encompassing; it is where we encounter high-vibrational qualities like compassion, love, courage, control, kindness, etc. I am connected to spirit and spirit gives me information through intuition. I engage in practices to keep my balance and keep the connection to spirit strong, just as I eat and exercise to keep my body strong. Without this connection it is much more difficult to climb out of roiling anger, agitation, depression and all of the other lower-vibrational qualities of life.

Many religions seem more divisive and dualistic than I am comfortable with dealing with either/or thinking. Holism is my religion.

The next chapter looks at some of the ways different belief structures and systems of thought can influence the way we experience the world and our sense of spirit.

CHAPTER FIVE

How Postmodern Thought Influences Reality Or Experience

I'm always amused when someone asks, "Do you believe in God?" and the reply is *yes* or *no*. I generally answer, "How much time do you have?" It requires much more than a simple yes or no answer and the very question gives short shrift to both the complexity and enormity of the relationship.

How we think influences what we believe. This means that as thought changes with the addition of new information, beliefs change as well. Whether the thoughts are true is not the point: belief can result from falsehood as well as fact. Take for example the changing beliefs that emerged based on people's changing thoughts about the shape of the world. When most people thought the earth was flat, this false information provided a useful basis for shaping beliefs about how far from home it was safe to travel. If people thought that the earth ended at some point beyond the horizon, then they believed they could only travel so far before being swallowed by the abyss. But thought evolved and by the time of Columbus most educated people thought that the earth was indeed spherical.[1] As thought changed, belief followed: people began to believe that since the earth was spherical, they could travel endlessly.

Throughout history, thoughts have shaped belief and ultimately how reality is perceived. Under the umbrella of different schools of thought (Platonic, Aristotelian, Newtonian, and more) emerged different beliefs and different perceptions of reality. These perceptions can apply to personal matters as well as cosmic. In an article in the *Huffington Post*, Lauren Schumacher explains that the Newtonian principle that "every action has an equal and opposite reaction," when applied to personal realities, can explain why love can be so hurtful.[2] You open your heart and sometimes an equal and opposite reaction occurs. (And in fact, I prefer believing that a failed love was the result of Newton's principle as opposed to my being unlovable.)

In my case, postmodern thought shifted my beliefs and brought me closer to my understanding of God. This

---

[1] The myth that Europeans around the time of Columbus believed the world was flat was popularized in the late nineteenth and early twentieth century, largely because of Washington Irving's fictionalized biography of Columbus, which suggested that most people at the time thought the world was flat and the trip couldn't be made. It has since been acknowledged that at the time of Columbus most educated people as well as most Christians believed that the world was round.

[2] Lauren Schumacher, "Newtonian Principles of the Heart," *Huffington Post* (blog), January 13, 2013, https://www.huffingtonpost.com/lauren-schuhmacher/newtonian-principles-of-t_b_2124229.html/.

process took some time, research and deep thought, not to mention practice. A lot of people are scared by the term "postmodernism." Perhaps a look at some related terms could help clarify it.

In the **premodern** period, which lasted until roughly the year 1650, Truth was revealed or handed down from higher authorities, like God or the church or ancient tradition. A religious or spiritual expression of this mode of thought might lead one to subscribe to an unquestioned faith based on a set of religious beliefs with the church acting as the final word based upon God's revelations. In this time, according to Karen Armstrong, the existence of God was not only universally accepted, questioning the existence of God was dangerous and potentially deadly.

The **modern** period, which lasted from the 1650s through the mid-twentieth century, lent itself to more questioning as to the nature of God. Science and reason began to assert that Truth was not to be received without question but needed to be uncovered by careful inquiry. Since God could not be proved through the scientific method, a shift in authority occurred, and both atheism and agnosticism became more prevalent. Karen Armstrong thinks that atheism should be looked at seriously as a condition revealing that current notions of God or religion are not working for the person. She believes that atheism should open conversation, not close it.[3]

After the Second World War, **postmodernism** came

---

[3] See Armstrong, *A History of God.*

on the scene. Postmodernism encouraged us to question previous approaches to knowing, and whenever possible to draw on multiple ways of knowing, including the premodern ways (revelation) and modern ways (science and reason), as well as intuitive, relational, and spiritual ways of knowing. Postmodern approaches push back against traditional sources of power and authority, and as a result, they are less hierarchical. Within this paradigm God can move from the man in the sky to a more abstract or mystical God—one who is felt and known experientially and does not necessarily fit into any neat box.[4]

Much postmodern thinking emerged from the world of physics and quantum physics, which opened up a new way of thinking about reality. The English physicist Sir James Jeans (1877–1946) said:

The essential fact is simply that *all* the pictures which science now draws of nature, which alone seem capable of according with observational fact are *mathematical* pictures. Most scientists would agree that they are nothing more than pictures—fictions, if you like, if by fiction you mean that science is not yet in contact with ultimate reality. Many would hold that, from the broad philosophical standpoint, the outstanding achievement of the twentieth-century physics is not the theory of relativity with its welding together of space and time, or the theory of quanta with

[4] For more on these paradigms, see Louis Hoffman, "Premodernism, Modernism, and Postmodernism: An Overview," *Postmodern Psychology*, March 14, 2017. http://postmodernpsychology.com/premodernism-modernism-postmodernism-an-overview/.

its present apparent negation of the laws of causation, or the dissection of the atom with the resultant discovery that things are not what they seem; it is the general recognition that we are not yet in contact with ultimate reality.[5]

Since the language of physics is mathematics, the "reality" physics speaks of is largely symbolic. Meaning resides within us. On a personal level this thinking can loosen the grip of fixed or absolute reality and allow for much more manipulation of information. As we look closer at postmodern thought and quantum physics we can see that the move from anthropomorphic God to Transcendent God becomes more flexible.

Postmodernism also introduces the notion of relativity and subjectivity into our mode of thought, tearing down the boundaries between the subjective and objective. Erwin Schrödinger described this erosion of boundaries:

[T]his boundary, so we are told, is not a sharp boundary at all. We are given to understand that we never observe an object without its being modified or tinged by our own activity in observing it. We are given to understand that under the impact of our refined methods of observation and of thinking about the results of our experiments that mysterious boundary between the subject and the object has broken down.[6]

Schrödinger took this a step further to suggest that reality itself is shaped by our perspectives:

---

[5] Wilber, *Quantum Questions*, 135.
[6] Wilber, *Quantum Questions*, 81.

[T]he idea of subjectivity in all appearance is very old and familiar. What is new in that present setting is this: that not only would the impressions we get from our environment largely depend on the nature and contingent state of our sensorium, but inversely, the very environment that we wish to take in is modified by us, notably by the devices we set up in order to observe it.[7]

As Deepak Chopra says, "The observer plays an active part in what he observes. We live in participatory universe."[8] Once the subject/object boundaries are blurred or broken, we are left with the idea that all is relative and there may or may not be absolutes. We now embrace that we are both changed by what we experience and that we change it in turn; as we are freed up to think about things differently, our beliefs are impacted in turn.

Does this blurring of subject/object boundaries mean that there are no longer absolutes? If you live long enough, you learn that the supposed absolute of accepted Truth is always evolving. I remember the years when science told us that fat was bad and that we should be eating margarine instead of butter. Twenty or so years later science tells us that margarine is bad for us, and we should be eating butter. Our understanding of the world evolves and changes, so in that respect there are no absolutes. But that just goes so far. We all agree that those tall structures with leaves on branches and trunks connecting them to the earth are

---

[7] Wilber, *Quantum Questions*, 81.
[8] Chopra, *The Future of God*, 135.

trees (or whatever word your language applies to those particular structures), and that they make their own food through photosynthesis. I would say that is absolute. That is true. But no two of us have the same relationship with trees. I grew up in Brooklyn and suffered from lack of sunlight during the winter months. I longed for daylight savings time and as soon as I saw the first buds on the trees outside my windows my mood lifted. Today I live in sunny southern California, where gray overcast days no longer alter my mood, but I still love trees. I live among trees with the ocean a mere three blocks away. I appreciate this idyllic setting and I love the ocean, but it is the trees that give me solace, that I am deeply connected to. So while there is universal agreement that some things are absolutely what we say they are, I will maintain that there are no absolutes. A tree is a tree. A rose is a rose. Absolutely. But how I think about, experience, and relate to them, is strictly between the tree and me, the rose and me.

Physicist Sir Arthur Eddington (1882–1944) wrote about this in terms of symbolic knowledge vs. intimate knowledge. He argued that "the more customary forms of reasoning have been developed for symbolic knowledge only." Intimate knowledge, however—personal, immediate, and experiential understanding—"will not submit to codification and analysis, or, rather, when we attempt to analyze it the intimacy is lost and it is replaced by symbolism."[9] In other words, there is no reasoned way

---

[9] Wilber, *Quantum Questions*, 207.

to interpret my relationship to trees. The tree itself can be easily examined and brought into the realm of symbolic knowledge, but my relationship with the tree is intimate knowledge. The idea of postmodernism leads us to an understanding that mystery tends to prevail when it comes to things of great importance to us; those things do not lend themselves to analysis, and if analyzed become symbolic, thereby losing the intimacy of the experience.

He uses the idea of humor to bring this home. Consider the difference between a joke and a laugh. The joke can be analyzed in many ways. Is it an ethnic joke, a domestic joke, a self-deprecating joke, a racist joke, silly slapstick, etc. The laugh is quite another thing. It cannot be analyzed.

And like the laugh, the immediate experience of God cannot be analyzed. Under a postmodern system of thought, the premodern notion of an anthropomorphic God—a man in the sky with a clear authority over all he created—can be modified. Even if one insists on projecting human qualities onto this God, his relationship to those qualities becomes more fluid. I might find myself deciding that a punitive God does not work as well for me as a just God and co-create a new relationship with a God based upon that quality. As my understanding of postmodernism deepened, my image of "God" faded to gray. Gone was the blinding white. God, the throne, the robes, beard, hair and clouds—all became stormy gray.

Some physicists say that we easily value "unexplainably meaningful experiences." We certainly allow a lot to go unquestioned and accepted. But for some reason when it comes to the experience of the divine, we want proof. And while religion can be analyzed, the mystery of the intimate experience of God cannot. Hopefully moving forward we will hold as high an expectation of "proving" the existence of a Higher Power as we hold of "proving" the existence of a love mechanism, or the meaning of trees, or any other of the intimate experiences we all have but have trouble explaining. In *The Future of God*, Deepak Chopra says that just as stars, galaxies, mountains, trees, and the sky cannot be objectively validated, neither can God. You may say that this rock feels hard or you may say you feel God's love. But one statement is not more or less true than the other.

I believe that quantum thought and postmodernism is bringing more and more people closer to understanding this. I think that postmodernism opens up the possibility for new relationships between who we are and what we observe or experience. I have a natural inclination toward respecting authority, but postmodern thinking has allowed me to assume my own authority in many ways. I feel a more cooperative relationship with doctors, lawyers, and all the specialists (authorities) I encounter—when I used to mostly accept their word as absolute. Now I am able to weigh what they say, counter with my own thoughts, and come to a more considered conclusion. I am still a great respecter of authority, but I cherry-pick. I have read dozens of books during my studies and yet refer to only the ones who stimulated my thinking, resonated what I already think, or opened me up to entirely new ways of looking at what I thought I understood. It is subtle, but empowering.

Nonetheless, I still have difficulty with some aspects of this mode of thinking. I am used to seeing the table upon which my computer rests as solid, as solid as the concrete I walk upon. My reality, formed by my beliefs, is material and densely real. Even when reduced to individual parts, those parts are solid. Then powerful microscopes and imaging tools tell us that the table, as well as the concrete, are not at all solid, but are composed of parts in constant motion—and that there is more empty space in these items than physical matter. It is still difficult for me to grasp this new way of thinking about the physical world. I hope that my grandchildren who were born into this modern understanding will be ready to accept the next leap of understanding once better tools of measurement are invented.

CHAPTER SIX

BELIEFS DWELL WITHIN WORLDVIEW AND CAN BE CHANGED WITH WILL AND INTENTION

Sometimes a word pokes at you. The word "postmodern" appeared to me over and over. Book and movie reviews described this piece or that as postmodern. The idea seemed complex, perhaps too difficult to understand. But it kept coming up as something I thought I should get to know better, and it ultimately was crucial to the development of my personal theology. Postmodernism's blurring of lines that I had once drawn in black and white brought me to the notion of a more abstract God—and in fact I don't think you can form a personal theology that includes a working relationship with God without going beyond the idea of an anthropomorphic God. For me, the "post" in postmodern is linked to transcendence—to going beyond. So in a subtle way my understanding of postmodernism allowed me to move beyond my seemingly indelible image of God as a superman in the sky.

Now, I do not for a second think that postmodern thought is the only way towards understanding a more abstract God! It was the trigger for me, but there can be many others. As I began to doubt my understanding about many things I previously thought I understood, I was ripe for moving into a new way of seeing the world. For me, postmodernism turned out to be that way.

But transformative experiences can come in many forms. Transformative experiences refer to those that lie beyond the realm of ordinary perception or beyond the limits of material existence. These experiences carry with them an extraordinary quality of numinosity, divinity, or grace, transporting us out of our ordinary worldview. I had this experience when I realized that something was guiding me *toward* finding health in a way that I feel I wouldn't have arrived at without help. It was a strange feeling, one that Marilyn Schlitz describes well in *Living Deeply*:

Transformation implies a change in the sense of self. There's both an inner and an outer dimension to it. It requires inner work and an appreciation for how that connects to being in the world, and the outer work of action and service. Transformation involves multiple dimensions of a person: our self-concept, the way in which we relate to other people, how we see the world, and what we feel is worth doing. Transformation really touches every aspect of our lives and has a lot to do with changing values. Transformation is multidimensional. It involves the heart, mind and spirit, and affects behavior and relationships in the world.[1]

---

[1] Schlitz, Vieten, and Amorok, *Living Deeply*, 20.

"Trans" means "going beyond." And as the above quote suggests, trans-formation involves not only a change in a specific behavior, or a specific aspect of a relationship, but an all-encompassing change resulting in a new expression of self.

I had to go beyond what I knew to understand the things that were puzzling me and to find a way to become holistically healthy. In *Kitchen Table Wisdom*, Naomi Remen describes transformation as a permanent shift in experience—one that happens sometimes spontaneously, sometimes after years of practice, sometimes in times of crisis. In my case it was brought about by crisis: two unrelated cancers eight years apart. This kind of experience, Remen says, shifts a person's values, often shuffling them like a deck of cards so that a value that's been on the bottom of the deck for many years emerges as the top card and becomes the guiding principle of a person's life from this moment on. Spirituality was most definitely on the bottom of my deck—but now it has become my ruling principle.

Transformation is more than mere change. Change requires trial, error and correction. How many times have we tried to change a habit? It takes patience and discipline. While we often stay on the new path for a while, it is easy to slip back into familiar behaviors, and then we have to take stock and move forward again. Sometimes the new behavior becomes habit, sometimes we try to tackle the same problems for decades. The process is difficult. Transformation can come from discipline and repeated practice, but it is pretty instantaneous when it happens. In terms of long-term practice, I could never have predicted what my *drills* for becoming a more generous person would reap, and for many years I did not actually *feel* the rewards. Now giving is perhaps one of my most joyous actions. Pressure transforms coal into diamonds, but while the diamond may contain the coal it is a completely different object after the transformation. I now take joy in giving. And it is unlikely that I will lose my spiritual connection now that I have found it.

We are about to see that changing one's beliefs is huge. And that is what I have been about for the past decade. I needed a spiritual connection to become well, only to discover that I needed a spiritual connection to do just about everything better than I had been. I needed a way to include some sort of God into this transformation because it became too difficult not to. To make that happen, I had to change my belief that God was a man in the sky. It was difficult and slow, but that image is fading—if slowly and with difficulty.

As Shakti Parwha Kaur Khalsa, an American-born woman who has become a Sikh and Kundalini yoga teacher, said: "We have embedded patterns of thought and behavior that we're not even aware of—and yet, they manifest in our daily lives, actions, and relationships."[2] These embedded beliefs run deep. For instance, I could never eat dog unless I was actually starving. My dogs are my family. I just couldn't

---

[2] Schlitz, Vieten, and Amorok, *Living Deeply*, 102.

do it, but in other countries dogs are raised and eaten as food like rabbits or chickens. Other embedded patterns of belief shape your political outlook. If you believe that you are likely to be involved in an attack by foreign terrorists you might develop the belief that immigrants and refugees coming into your country are dangerous, because there might be a terrorist among them. If you do not believe that terrorism is a great threat you might look at these people differently. You might have a different worldview, one more compassionate than fearful.

Our beliefs can have direct impact on our lives and health. Just look at the placebo effect. In a statistically significant number of cases, patients who take a sugar pill experience a reduction in their symptoms. This would seem to prove that belief, expectation, and intention can be as effective in treating disease as outside intervention. At the same time, beliefs can harm us—the placebo effect has its counterpart in the "nocebo effect": the expectation that a treatment will not be effective often turns out to be a self-fulfilling prophecy. Negative beliefs have the power to damage our health.[3]

How can we change the worldview and our beliefs? Not through facts. Marshaling facts and logical arguments makes no difference to embedded beliefs: As David Corcoran has put it: "When the facts get in the way of our

_____

[3] For more on the "nocebo" effect, see Bruce Lipton, *The Biology of Belief: Unleashing the Power of Consciousness, Matter, and Miracles* (Carlsbad: Hay House, 2015), 164ff.

beliefs, our brains are marvelously adept at dispensing with the facts." [4] My inability to eat dog is not based on facts; I can eat rabbit without a qualm, but not dog, even though there is really little difference. It seems that people also often choose beliefs over facts in the rearing of children. A child does something that interferes with your image of them and you ignore or bury it rather than confront it. Many people choose to ignore the fact that there have been almost no terrorist attacks by foreigners in this country, still insisting foreigners are dangerous. And since facts can't make a dent in those beliefs, will and intention must be engaged in order to change them.

Will and intention are essential to developing new beliefs as well as the development of a personal theology. Beliefs are both entrenched and malleable—in order to move them you need intention and then the will to stick with it. Will is that drive that pushes you to the finish line even when it is difficult to get there. It is the drive that keeps you on a chosen path even when it seems almost impossible. Intention is the explication of what you wish to accomplish. When I do healing touch, I express my intention at the beginning of each session to establish healing in the highest interest of my client. Intention is throwing out into the universe what you want or desire and if your intention is in alignment with your highest self

[4] David Corcoran, ed., *The New York Times Book of Science: More than 150 Years of Groundbreaking Scientific Coverage* (New York: Sterling, 2015), 209.

you can expect a pretty good outcome. I equate intention with prayer.

So what specifically can we *do*?

We can change our worldview through accessing the unconscious. There are various ways of accessing our unconscious and the embedded patterns of thought and belief it contains: for example, we can record and study our dreams, meditate, or through the use of imagery and visualization. No matter what method we use, however, the point is it takes will and intention to get to the bottom of our beliefs.

And we can do it through harnessing our emotions. Bruce Lipton tells us that beliefs act like filters on a camera which change how we see the world: change the filter and you change the view. And, Lipton tells us, we can change the filter: we have some control over our emotions, and since emotions affect beliefs we have control over our beliefs. I want to make it clear that beliefs are both entrenched and malleable because the power to change the world by changing a belief is extraordinary. And it's really important that we find the will and intention to make those changes because, now more than ever, the divisions in our country are deep and broad.

I think if I had to describe my religion I would call myself a Pragmatic Holist. I always look for the holistic solution and can usually eventually get there. But this country's politics are leaving me at a loss right now. I'm beginning to see that when we argue about divisive issues we are often having the wrong argument. And although we are labeling this division as democrat vs. republican, or conservative vs. liberal, I'm not certain that it isn't really about something else. I just haven't gotten to the source of this conflict yet.

It reminds me a bit of the abortion issue and the long drawn-out struggle over abortion and reproductive rights. I came of age at a time when abortion was illegal. Fear of pregnancy colored all male-female teenage relationships to some degree: pregnancy could lead to great physical risk if an illegal abortion was chosen, or shame if the pregnancy was carried to term. Birth control was not always readily available and besides, sex outside of marriage was still considered not the best idea. When *Roe v. Wade* was decided by the Supreme Court in 1973 and abortions became legal, a lot of things changed. We had greater access to the pill and other easy-to-use forms of birth control. We had a sexual revolution as a result, but surprisingly the number of abortions went steadily down after abortions became legal. According the Guttmacher Institute (an organization that supports legal abortion), in 1980 there were 29.3 abortions per 1000 women; by 2014 that number had been cut in half, to 14.6. The people who believe abortion to be wrong are fighting to overturn *Roe v. Wade*. The people who believe in a woman's right to choose are fighting to keep abortion legal. The argument has resulted in a slow deterioration of the number of abortion facilities, but abortion is still legal.

And yet I think we are having the wrong argument.

It is an either/or argument and entirely dualistic. And yet we persist in order to hold tightly to beliefs that may no longer be entirely relevant. No one thinks an abortion is a great idea. In my opinion we can eliminate most of the need for abortion if we change the conversation and focus on serious sex education for preteens, our less than realistic views of teenagers and their sexuality, and education about money—how much it takes to live and how to manage it. We need to have more conversation about violence against women and incest. There is always a way to cross even a divide as entrenched as the abortion issue. I think the real discussion is how to avoid unwanted pregnancies.

But as the old story of the Hatfields and McCoys reminds us, feuds resulting from entrenched beliefs are not easily softened. Addressing these intractable issues takes will, staying with the discussion even when it is difficult, and intention (which I see as the statement of an agreed-upon vision). Forming a new belief system or personal theology requires developing a working relationship between will, intention, and belief. Doing this has allowed me to create an active and vibrant theology out of mostly antagonistic beliefs. To create some kind of bridge between this current political divide requires the same challenge and work.

So in order to change a belief you must engage will and intention and recognize that you are seeing things through a particular worldview. But first you must be aware and that is where consciousness enters the conversation.

CHAPTER SEVEN

IS CONSCIOUSNESS DEVELOPMENTAL AND CAN ONE CHANGE ONE'S LEVEL OF CONSCIOUSNESS?

Consciousness is a big concept and one that is not widely understood. I have concluded that there is big-*C* consciousness and little-*c* consciousness which I will try to describe here. I will also attempt a linear explanation to expand the concept and to give the reader another view of consciousness. I will also give two anecdotes about how bringing information from my unconscious into consciousness enabled me to change some false beliefs that were pretty entrenched.

We are all familiar with the idea that our own particular personal consciousness—our awareness and sense of self—can be expanded or enlarged by allowing information from our unconscious to emerge into consciousness. (We will talk more about the various processes that can help us do that in a future chapter.)

At the same time, consciousness is not a purely individual matter. Physicist Erwin Schrödinger sees human consciousness as tied to each individual but also connected to something much greater.

Consciousness finds itself intimately connected with, and dependent on, the physical state of a limited region of matter, the body. (Consider the changes of mind during the development of the body, as puberty, aging, dotage, etc. or consider the effects of fever, intoxication, narcosis, lesion of the brain and so on.) Now, there is a greater plurality of similar bodies. Hence the pluralization of consciousness or minds seems a very suggestive hypothesis. Probably all simple ingenuous people, as well as the great majority of western philosophers, have accepted it. It leads almost immediately to the invention of souls, as many as there are bodies, and to the question whether they are mortal as the body is or whether they are immortal and capable of existing by themselves.[1]

Schrödinger says that although we experience consciousness only as individuals and never directly experience a consciousness other than our own, this is not to say that each of us individually has a consciousness (or soul) that is distinct and separate from all others. Instead, he says, all our individual consciousnesses—the "plurality of similar bodies"—can be thought of as manifestations or reflections of a single larger awareness. In other words, I have my own personal consciousness to work with and may also draw upon a kind of universal consciousness.

This universal consciousness binds us together. As

---

[1] Wilber, *Quantum Questions*, 94.

Einstein points out:

A human being is part of a whole, called by us "universe," a part limited in time and space. He experiences himself, his thoughts and feelings as something separated from the rest:

...a kind of optical delusion of his consciousness. This delusion is a kind of prison for us, restricting us to our personal desires and to affection for a few persons nearest to us. Our task must be to free ourselves from this prison by widening our circle of compassion to embrace all living creatures and the whole of nature in its beauty.[2]

Once again we are pointed in the direction of connection; that our separateness is an illusion and that natural law suggests that we are deeply connected. I am aware that as my own consciousness has expanded, my connection to all living things has grown, as has my connection to nature.

In the most general terms I would say that *Consciousness* (with a big *C*) is this universal consciousness and connectedness—all the knowledge that is; and *consciousness* (with a little *c*) is our own particular personal consciousness, which contains that which we are aware of. It is my experience that practices that help us expand our consciousness work in both directions: they connect us to our individual unconscious and they also help draw information from universal consciousness. Sitting quietly in my chair after my lymphoma diagnosis, I received the

---

[2] Schlitz, Vieten, and Amorok, *Living Deeply*, 175.

message to give the cancer to my doctor and figure out how to be healthy. That information, which I have called divine, came to me through this expanded consciousness— through connection to my own unconscious and to a broader consciousness. I received the information that I had to get healthy from my own small-*c* consciousness and the way to get healthy from big-*C* Consciousness.

As seekers, there are various tools we can use to assess our own growth. Back in chapter 2, we looked at Deepak Chopra's hierarchical way of understanding a relationship to God. Here we will turn to Ken Wilber's "Great Chain of Being," (sometimes called a "Great Nest"), which can be visualized as a series of concentric circles. The smallest circle represents matter and physics; the next one out is biology/life; then psychology/mind; then theology/soul; then the largest, most encompassing circle of mysticism/ spirit. The key to the Great Chain of Being is that each circle allows you to accurately see or measure only those things that are within it: a "lower" or inner level cannot be used to measure a "higher," outer level. This means that you cannot measure the soul using the same tools that you use to measure mind or matter, and you can only get an accurate view of the whole from the outermost level of mysticism/spirit.[3]

---

[3] See Wilber, *Quantum Questions.*

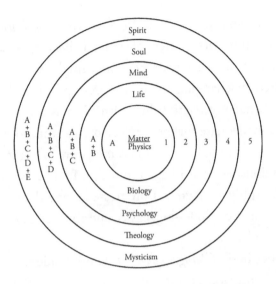

[Image from Ken Wilber, *A Brief History of Everything*: Boston, Shambhala Publications, Inc., 2001.]

This chart is valuable because it allows us to look at complex information in a linear fashion—to give our left brains a chance to come to terms with this very right-brain material.

Looking at consciousness in terms of levels (like Chopra) or layers in the "nest" (like Wilber) allows you to place yourself so you can see where you have been and where you might go. In addition, it helps you see where others are on the ladder, which can smooth relations. If you are on an outer or upper level having a discussion with someone on an inner or lower level it is probably safest to keep the conversation on the level you are both comfortable in to avoid both friction and misunderstanding. Knowing what level you are on can also give you a window into understanding the source of your beliefs and perhaps inform you on what your next step might be if you are interested in changing them. For example, I understood early on that my relationship with God as a man in the sky was inadequate for me. I rejected an anthropomorphic God, but it was only when I became aware of higher levels of consciousness that I began to realize I had the ability to make God bigger. And as I progressed along the stages, so did my vision of God—bigger became abstract and abstract became holistic.

In her book *Changes of Mind*, Jenny Wade talks about stages of consciousness in much the same way that others have characterized children's developmental stages. Wade gives us twelve stages of consciousness development and lays out the assumptions for each stage and transition. I will not go deeply into the assumptions of each stage, but the names of the stages are telling. Each of us exists mostly in one stage—most adults occupy the Conformist stage of consciousness—but we have elements of all stages within us and we can move from one stage to another if we wish. Each of these stages has a list of assumptions about the behaviors common to that particular stage. I list the primary motivation of each stage.[4]

---

[4] Jenny Wade, *Changes of Mind: A Holonomic Theory of the Evolution of Consciousness* (Albany: State University of New York Press, 1996).

Stage of Consciousness	Primary Motivation
1. Prenatal and Perinatal Consciousness	None/avoid discomfort/ survival
2. Reactive Consciousness	Cessation of discomfort
3. Naïve Consciousness	Physical security and safety
4. Egocentric Consciousness	Survival of the mental ego as self
5. Conformist Consciousness	Safety and security through predictability
6. Achievement Consciousness	Personal success that is socially recognized
7. Affiliative Consciousness	Belonging in close harmonious relationships
8. Authentic Consciousness	Personal growth for its own sake
9. Transcendent Consciousness	Transcending the egoic self to grasp the absolute
10. Unity Consciousness	None—merely living in the Ground of All Being
11. After-Death Consciousness	Obligation to return to incarnate life to complete unfinished business

This is a powerful model for understanding how consciousness affects beliefs. Note that the earlier stages are concerned with self-protection; it follows that beliefs formed at these stages of development might be based upon fear of personal harm. This would explain beliefs that are racist or xenophobic. A person who cannot think symbolically will most likely adopt a literal interpretation of the Bible. A person who lives mostly in egocentric consciousness might well be threatened by ideas that transcend ego. Understanding these levels brings greater understanding of the way people see the world. And, just as important, these levels can be useful in assessing the evolution of your own particular consciousness.

This feeds into my discussion in the previous chapter about having the wrong arguments about issues we are intractable on. My ideas about abortion were shaken when in Wades's book I read about examples of very early fetal awareness. In short if a needle is injected into a pregnant woman, even a very young fetus, whose eyes are closed and who cannot hear, will withdraw its body from the approaching needle. Later, when the fetus has arms that can move, it will strike at the needle. I guess that is some kind of embryonic awareness. So my argument about pro-choice or anti-choice changes with this information. No longer is that embryo a lump of cells to me; I feel differently about abortion than I did before. With more information my argument became wobbly and as I understood more about consciousness my argument changed so that I focus now on finding better ways of avoiding unwanted pregnancy rather than focusing on choice.

Here is a story of my own *ascending consciousness*. I lived in a cult for nineteen years and have often wondered why, even when things were going badly, I did not leave. What I now understand is that I was firmly in Conformist

Consciousness—as long as the other members went along, I did as well. I took my cues from my peers because identification with the group was primary. As long as my closest friends stayed in the group, I quickly dismissed the idea of leaving even at my unhappiest. But when the people closest to me began jumping ship and leaving the community, I found it easy to do so as well. Not long after I left this community, my husband and I started a business. I began to educate myself and ultimately wound up as a graduate student. During this period, I was firmly in Achievement Consciousness. As a result of my newly acquired knowledge, however, I began needing a new group of like-minded people, leading me to Affiliative Consciousness. And after continuing my study and growth I am moving into Authentic Consciousness. I have had glimpses of Transcendent Consciousness—and although I do believe that I can achieve that, I question just how far up the ladder one can climb from one's starting point. Each step along the path was to some degree a struggle; the movement toward new and more like-minded people brought about changes in friendship that were not always easy. I often feel the pull back toward conformity, especially in wanting my *friends* from earlier phases of my life to recognize and accept the changes in me. They don't and won't. The transitions are not smooth and can even be painful.

But as Marion Woodman, the famous Jungian psychoanalyst, has said, not every one who ages becomes wise. Becoming wise requires work—you have to access your unconscious and expand your consciousness.[5] Sometimes sharp turns on the road of life lead us towards that work. Leaving the cult, having a couple of cancers that I had to figure out—these events informed me that my awareness was limited and I began searching for ways to gain greater understanding of my life. But it is not easy.

Two examples from my own life show how my own shift in consciousness allowed me to alter false beliefs. They show how deeply embedded false beliefs can be, how a release of information from the unconscious to facilitate expanded consciousness can lead to a change in beliefs, and how intention rules the process.

My mother used to warn me against getting above myself. She would say things like "get off your high horse, young lady," and "just who do you think you are?" and "you're getting too big for your britches." Perhaps that is why I have often sabotaged my own attempts to reach loftier goals, or at least feel somewhat ashamed of wanting more than I "should."

In college I got engaged, but there was no money for jewels—and I was one of the only girls in my class not to receive an engagement ring. One other young woman in my class also did not have a ring for a while because her boyfriend did not have the money—until one fine day she walked into class with a large oval-cut diamond ring that her

---

[5] Marion Woodman, *The Crown of Age: The Rewards of Conscious Aging*, read by the author (Sounds True Audio, 2004).

parents had bought for them. I overheard her whispering that she wondered how I would feel about her getting a ring. At the time I thought the diamond superfluous and way out of reach and no big deal. But I guess being left out and the feeling that I was *less than* left its mark, because several decades later, as soon as I had a few extra dollars, I bought myself a lovely diamond ring—just to show that I had attained membership in a club I didn't even know I wanted to join. When I lived in the intentional community money was scarce because we lived communally, sharing cars, furniture and meals. I never thought about jewelry. When I left I wanted to conform to my new community and having a diamond ring fit right in. It was only when I began to understand concepts like belief, thought, and consciousness that I was able to question these choices.

I struggled with similar feelings when I was about to put my ideas together to write this book. I was completely disabled by the false belief that I was getting "too big for my britches." What was I thinking? Who did I think I was? I believed that I could only accomplish so much and no more—taking on a book project was way more than my mother would be comfortable with. It impacted my confidence, my voice and certainly my choices.

At the time, I was not aware of the source of these beliefs and behaviors. But as I engaged in processes and activities to bring my unconscious to light, I became more aware. I began to wear my diamond ring less and somehow my ideas for this book came together in such a way that I could actually begin writing. These were small obstacles—needing a diamond ring to prove that I am okay is not the end of the world—but I think I limited myself for much of my life with these deeply embedded false beliefs. These self-limiting beliefs were not in my consciousness. It was only when I began altering ordinary consciousness that these beliefs took form and I was able to work with them.

My personal experience illuminates only a sliver of the understanding of consciousness. Psychiatrist Stanislav Grof says that consciousness can be studied, but in the absence of direct experience, this is a bit like reading about the taste of a strawberry rather than tasting it directly.[6]

The mind does not shine by its own light
It too is an object, illuminated by the Self…
But the Self is boundless.
It is the pure Consciousness that illumines the content of the mind…
Egoism, the limiting sense of "I," results from the Individual intellect attributing the power of Consciousness to itself.[7]

[6] Stanislav Grof, *The Cosmic Game: Explorations of the Frontiers of Human Consciousness,* (New York: State University of New York Press, 1998).
[7] Roger Walsh and Frances Vaughan, eds., *Paths Beyond Ego: The Transpersonal Vision* (New York, Penguin, 1993), 14.

Before we return to a discussion about my new big relationship with God we need to look at some of the processes, practices, and modalities that alter consciousness so that it can expand.

CHAPTER EIGHT

ALTERED STATES LEAD TO EXPANDED CONSCIOUSNESS AND EXPANDED CONSCIOUSNESS ALTERS BELIEFS

Developing a strong spiritual connection that opens a channel for new information requires practice, and these spiritual practices take time. But the question of how we spend our time is complicated. My friend will not read during the day: it would indicate that she is lazy. My husband will not look at a TV during the day (unless it is his beloved UCLA Bruins playing basketball—and even then only on Saturday or Sunday). Watching TV during the day would be a waste of time. A woman in my meditation class admitted that she could make time to meditate once a day but simply couldn't see her way to doing it twice. My husband leaned over and asked me how much time I thought she spent on the Internet. We are in many ways ruled by time; how we spend it shapes who we are. But in our culture spending time on practices designed to help us go inward is often frowned upon or dismissed as *navel-gazing*—though perhaps the growing popularity of mindfulness is encouraging more people to change that.

So it is important to understand that engaging in spiritual practices will take time, and that this is time you have to make—because without these practices it is almost impossible to move towards a strong spiritual connection.

ALTERED STATES

The point of spiritual practice is to create an altered state of consciousness. While this sounds esoteric, it is actually a very pragmatic thing to do (as I have already said, my religion can best be described as Holistic Pragmatism). In *Spiritual Solutions,* Deepak Chopra tells us that the solution to a problem can never be found on the level of the problem. So when we are roiling in mass confusion it makes little sense to try to find a solution within that situation. You have a problematic work relationship with your boss, but you need your income. No matter how many ways you look at the situation, as long as you are working from within the situation, solutions are hard to see. In order to find these solutions, we must go to a different state of consciousness than the *ordinary.* As Chopra puts it elsewhere: "In a sudden expansion of consciousness, the mask of the material world falls away, revealing hidden meaning."[1] (Don't worry—this sounds far more complicated than it is!)

An altered state of consciousness is simply a state of consciousness that is not your ordinary state of consciousness. In order to enter an altered state you have

---

[1] Chopra, *The Future of God,* 66.

to destabilize the normal state of being. This can be done through singing, chanting, drumming, using mind-altering plants and herbs, ceremony, or ritual.[2] Charles Tart describes non-ordinary states of consciousness as denoting "alterations in both the content and pattern of the functioning consciousness" that allow us to see things differently and to see solutions that were previously hidden.[3] For me the arrival of such a solution is often something so simple and obvious that I feel like hitting my head with my hand and exclaiming, *"How could I have not seen that?"* It's actually a bit magical. Even though the new way you see things may feel normal—you may say, "Of *course* I should do X, Y, or Z!"—before that transformation happened X, Y, and Z were completely unavailable as solutions.

In the West, we mostly try to achieve altered mind-states through drugs; in fact, it has been said that in the western world *only* states of intoxication are recognized as mind altering. Our most traditional way of altering consciousness is with alcohol, but in many ways alcohol is mind-diminishing as opposed to mind-expanding. Other therapies, however, are gaining broader acceptance. For instance Charles Grob, a psychiatrist at UCLA, has found that psychedelics can be a useful therapeutic tool for patients, leading to reduced fear of death in terminally ill patients and relief from psychopathology. In healthy

---

[2] See Roger N. Walsh, *The Spirit of Shamanism* (New York: Perigee Books, 1990).
[3] Schlitz, Vieten, and Amorok, *Living Deeply*, 47-48.

volunteers, he has found that psychedelics lead to psychological insight, enhanced creativity, a reorientation of values toward less materialistic goals, and transformative spiritual experiences.[4] His research is controversial but also potentially promising.

Drugs, however, are not the only gateway. Native Americans make ritual use of mind-altering plants in ceremonies where "the soul of a person enters the spirit world for more intense communication with spirits including spirits of ancestors."[5] But this is not their only means of bringing about altered states of consciousness: they have many other ways of invoking spirits, including simply saying the name of the spirit, dancing, drumming, breathing, and sweat lodges. It may be that the absence of mind-altering ceremonies and rituals in our everyday Western lives contributes to or leads to the unintended consequence of illegal drug use.

Before we look at why practices are important, I want to dispel the notion that these practices and transformations are earth-shattering experiences. Mind-altering experiences range from esoteric to the commonplace. Shamanic healers travel to the underworld and overworld during their ceremonies and commune with spirits in both realms. But I simply meditate every day—there is not much drama, but I see transformational results. Similarly, the practices that

---

[4] Described in Schlitz, Vieten, and Amorok, *Living Deeply*, 51ff.
[5] Mircea Eliade, *From Primitives to Zen: A Thematic Sourcebook on the History of Religions* (New York: Harper & Row Publishers, 1967), 412.

bring about these experiences can be esoteric or entirely mundane. In the next section I will focus on the practices I have found work for me. They are no better or worse than others, but one cannot do them all, and the ones that call to you are probably the ones you should incorporate into your life. There are many reasons cultures engage in mind-altering activities and just the experience itself is often a good enough reason. I would like to add, from an evolutionary point of view, that the *drills* of my early life translated into the *practices* I now engage in. The drills were temporary activities intended to move me from point A to point B (as in the drills that helped me become more rather than less generous). The following practices, however, have no true goal other than expanding consciousness and they can be incorporated into daily life.

Practices

The word "practice" is both a verb and a noun. You can practice something in order to learn it—"I am practicing being open and honest with others"—and something can become your practice—"It is my practice to be forthcoming." Thus, practice is both the act of performing a set of exercises and the form, philosophy, or worldview underlying these exercises. Most commonly, practice is thought of as the act of repeating something over and over for the purpose of learning and gaining experience. In the course of our work, we have come to define transformative practice as any set of internal or external activities you engage in with the intention of fostering long-lasting shifts in the way you experience and relate to yourself and others.[6]

If you were born in India spiritual practice might well have been part of your education. When you were young, your family might have hired a guru to teach you spiritual laws and practices that would become as much a part of your life as brushing your teeth or eating breakfast. The teaching of spirituality is built into the culture even to the smallest detail. In our country spiritual practices are not part of everyone's everyday lives, nor are we comfortable with the vocabulary of spirituality. This is not to say we don't have such experiences—we all have "aha moments" of great insight, intuitive knowings, and transformative experiences that leave us thinking we will never be the same again. But many of us don't know what to do with them. Sometimes the experience is enjoyed for what it is and then let go. Some people do not even recognize what is happening and instead of exploring the experience explain it away, diminishing the impact. And some people, like me, say *I want more of this*. I want these types of experiences to become a norm in my life. I want my consciousness to expand to the point that intuitive knowing and information from *outside the box* is as available to me as what I read each day in the newspaper.

What can you expect from practice? In our culture, we tend to define transformative experiences as WOW experiences—like Fourth of July explosions. But some of

---

[6] Schlitz, Vieten, and Amorok, *Living Deeply*, 92–93.

these experiences can be very small; small, but still profound. Or our practice can simply prepare the ground, poising us to be ready for revelation when it comes. As Schlitz puts it, "Realization isn't something we can do, it's only something we can be ready for. Practice isn't the cause of realization, but it helps you be more open and ready to receive what the universe has to offer." And prepare the ground we must—our consciousness is not going to expand or evolve to a higher level on its own. After the intention to grow in this direction must come practices to enable that growth. The practices are like food for the soul and spirit. Another way of looking at the reason for practice is to "cultivate what we call the 'reshimu'—the subtle imprint that is left after the great opening."[7] This is another way of saying that while insights can fade quickly, practice can keep the *imprint* of those experiences alive. I like that imagery.

An example of such an imprint might be the sound of the Muslim call to prayer. I am not a Muslim and have never studied or practiced that religion, but when I hear the call to prayer in a recording or on television I stop to consider that millions are now praying. I am reminded of my spiritual connection even if I am simply cooking dinner. Once again, the authors of *Living Deeply* say it well.

One of the primary functions of many transformative practices is to reestablish the internal balance between ego and soul, mind and body, self and other, doing and being. These practices take the ego out of the driver's seat for a

---

[7] Schlitz, Vieten, and Amorok, *Living Deeply*, 66–67, 86.

while, and allow the many other parts of your being—your feeling self, your creative self, your intuitive self—to have a turn at the wheel.[8]

And that in itself is a great reason to pick a practice or two to add to your life.

There are thousands or millions of practices out there. The ones I am going to focus on can be divided into four basic types: Mind-Body-Spirit Interventions, Energy Therapies, Whole Medical Systems, and Creative/Ritual Practices.

Mind-Body-Spirit Interventions

These practices include meditation, relaxation, imagery, visualization, hypnosis, yoga, tai chi, prayer, art, music, dance therapies, cognitive-behavioral therapies, biofeedback, therapeutic counseling, aromatherapy, stress management, and journaling.[9] To some degree all these practices are designed to help us go inward, which helps us access information from higher realms.

Meditation: This is my primary practice. The obvious question surrounding our intention of expanding consciousness is how do we begin to look inward when the outer, material world is calling to us practically all of the time? The answer of course, is to set aside time to go inward by simply being quiet and embracing silence. A

---

[8] Schlitz, Vieten, and Amorok, *Living Deeply*, 119.
[9] For a more extensive list, see Lucia Thornton, *Whole Person Caring: An Interprofessional Model for Healing and Wellness*, (Indianapolis: Sigma Theta Tau International, 2013), 11.

useful definition comes from Rudolph Ballentine in his book *Radical Healing*:

Meditation is an activity that entails posture, sitting with spine upright in postures that vary from challenging to total comfort. It is an experience in being with one's self in stillness. The mind is active and thoughts are inevitable, but there are ways of bringing attention back from thoughts to the stillness. One technique is repeating a mantra, a one, two or three word repetitive phrase such as so hum which is a universal mantra. Some people follow the breath or focus on the place between the eyebrows. Meditation is a way of establishing a new relationship with yourself, extricating yourself from the chatter and busyness of the mental field.[10]

There are many forms of meditation and it has become a more and more common activity; many books and CDs are available to help you get started.

Deepak Chopra offers some helpful context for the beginner. He presents the following list of things he wished he knew about meditation when he started.

1. Meditation is natural. It's not an exotic import from the East and the cultural values of the East.

2. Meditation is about mind, body, and spirit as one continuous whole, not three separate things.

3. The benefits of meditation go deeper than we imagine. At the very least, genetic activity responds very quickly and substantially to meditation.

4. Meditation uncovers the true self that lies at the

---

[10] Ballentine, *Radical Healing*, 224.

core of every person.

5. The state of pure awareness that is reached through meditation is the ground state of everything.[11]

In my own case, I knew I needed to meditate long before I was actually able to do it. When I started it was impossible for me to sit for ten minutes. I tried setting the timer for five minutes and still felt as if I was going to jump out of my skin. For years I repeated the pattern, trying, failing, trying again, failing again, until finally after many years I discovered Primordial Sound Meditation which uses a personal mantra. Now, after many years, my head is no longer filled with useless chatter. My thoughts have gotten softer and softer, until now they largely take the form not of words but pictures. Just repeating my mantra can bring me back to stillness when my thoughts get loud.

This progress came slowly. At first meditating was a bit like exercise; I did it because it was good for me even though I did not love it. Now I can say in all honesty that I look forward to that peaceful, quiet time and when my timer gently chimes at twenty minutes I often shut it off and continue. I have no idea of why I stuck with something that was so difficult for over twenty years, but I'm glad I paid attention and did just that. My advice to others is to keep trying. If meditating on your own doesn't work, try a guided meditation; if you can't sit or don't want to,

---

[11] Deepak Chopra, "5 Things I Wish I Had Known When I Began Meditating," *The Chopra Center* (blog), https://chopra.com/articles/5-things-i-wish-i-had-known-when-i-began-meditating/.

try walking meditation. Whatever your needs or situation, there is probably a meditation style that will work for you.

Next we are going to bring imagination into focus as the foundation for the following practices.

Visualization and Imagery: Norris describes guided imagery as:

...a form of deliberate, directed daydreaming—a purposeful use of the imagination, using words and phrases designed to evoke rich, multisensory fantasy and memory, in order to create a deeply immersive, receptive mind-state that is ideal for catalyzing desired changes in mind, body, psyche, and spirit. For most people, imagery is an easy, user-friendly form of meditation that yields immediately felt results. Its gentle nature belies its potency and its research proven, cumulative efficacy.[12]

These methods allow us to tap into our unconscious and gain deeper understanding of ourselves. Since so much of our direction comes from our unconscious, all methods that allow us to communicate with that part of ourselves are valuable in the quest for fuller consciousness.

Imagery can also affect our actions and behaviors. It can help us quiet our minds, "settle down hypervigilant brain functioning and allow the higher brain to get back to doing its job."[13] We can visualize medicines working on parts of our bodies or we can visualize our dream job:

---

[12] Norris and Porter, *Why Me?*, 150.
[13] Belleruth Naparstek, *Invisible Heroes: Survivors of Trauma and How They Heal* (New York: Bantam Books, 2004), 157.

in both cases the images of these things can influence the direction our lives take.

I have used visualization and imagery quite a bit—both guided visualizations and some I created myself. When I was receiving treatment for lymphoma, I visualized the treatment traveling through my body, attaching to all of the cancer cells flowing through my lymphatic system and blood vessels and being stored in my spleen. In one visualization, I pictured my white blood cells rushing to my spleen, where millions of them packed the inside of the spleen and formed a sort of bandage that overflowed to the outside and wrapped itself around the organ. The next day I visualized unwrapping my spleen and removing the packing to do it all again. If nothing else this kind of visualization exercise is a productive way to spend the time you can't be doing much else, and it gives you some sense of control.

Massage: Massage used to be a much more routine part of patient therapy. There are different kinds of massage, and finding a good therapist—one who can sense what your body needs—is key. I always can tell when my body needs to be touched in that way and I can feel the stress leaving my muscles as my therapist works on me. My therapist is very sensitive. She always finds the spots that need extra time and attention, even without me telling her. So I don't have to do anything besides go into a delicious state of relaxation. Many think of massage as a luxury or purely sensual experience, but emotions and stress are often stored in the body and can be released from muscle, and tissue through massage. [14]

Yoga: Yoga is an increasingly popular form of exercise and spiritual practice—and there are both traditional and non-traditional styles available. For me, it was not a successful path to spiritual awakening, although I practiced traditional yoga for fourteen years. I am not physically flexible—I have never been able to touch my toes. And even though I became my class's prop queen, using blocks, belts, and blankets to enable the poses my body balked at, it still hurt. I was never able to respond to my teacher's command to *feel the ease in the pose.* What ease? Instead, I had constant lower back tension. It was not the right practice for me and I should have quit long before I did. I now do an exercise routine that is somewhat less mindful, but that doesn't hurt my body. I get my mindful activity elsewhere.

Journaling: Many people keep a journal of some kind as part of their spiritual practice. There are many styles of journaling. You can write for a specified period of time or number of pages. You can dialogue with another person, yourself, yourself as a child, your higher self. You can write letters to people living or dead. I have been journaling for years and yet when I am in the middle of a crisis I often forget. When my sister died, my therapist suggested I journal and it was on those pages that my psychic explosion took form and sorted itself out.

---

[14] See Thornton, *Whole Person Caring.*

Some write their journals on the computer, but I believe that handwriting is the best method. In the process of writing, interesting things happen between the brain and the hand—and what appears on the paper is often surprisingly informative. You can discover relationships and ways of seeing situations that were previously unavailable. Although many people save their journals, I don't. Periodically I look through them and tear out pages that I might want to remember, but most of it is rambling and I throw it away.

ENERGY THERAPIES

These include therapeutic touch, Reiki, qigong, acupressure, healing touch, Jyorei, Jin Shin Jyutsu, Pranic healing, light therapy, magnet therapy, and Feldenkreis.

Acupuncture: Acupuncture treats imbalances in the body, mind, or spirit by adjusting the flow of energy through the meridians of our bodies. Our bodies have hundreds of meridians or points that relate to both the physical body and emotions as well. The doctor places tiny needles along the meridians that are related to the challenged area of the body, mind or spirit. Sometimes I use acupuncture because my arm is sore or my lower back is tight, or for digestive problems. I used acupuncture and massage to treat arthritis in my hands a couple of years ago and my hands, three years later, have almost no swelling and are pain free. But mostly I use acupuncture when I am just *off*. Not long after my sister died and I was very much unbalanced I had a two-hour acupuncture session. When it was over I could absolutely feel a shift in my mood. These are powerful interventions.

Tai Chi and **Qigong:** These are Chinese traditions that deal with breath, balance, posture, stretching, and mindfulness. Tai chi is a noncompetitive martial arts tradition that has evolved over centuries to become a means of alleviating stress and anxiety—a form of "meditation in motion." Advocates claim that it promotes serenity and inner peace.[15] Qigong is an ancient Chinese health care system that integrates physical postures, breathing techniques and focused intention. The word *qigong* is made up of two Chinese words. *Qi* (pronounced chee) is usually translated to mean the life force or vital-energy that flows through all things in the universe; *gong* means cultivation or skill.[16] I tried Qigong but realized that the moves were so subtle that it would take me years to simply become competent let alone attain any semblance of mastery.

Healing Touch: There are several healing touch techniques and they deal with connecting and balancing major and minor chakras, techniques for alleviating pain, ones for headaches, back problems and mind clearing. One of the beauties of healing touch is that the practitioner as well as the patient are affected. How this

---

[15] Joseph Nordqvist, "What are the Health Benefits of Tai Chi?," *Medical News Today*, September 6, 2016, www.medicalnewstoday.com/articles/265507.php/.

[16] "What is Qigong?," National Qigong Association, https://www.nqa.org/what-is-qigong-/.

works is complicated and not well researched as yet, but the grounded practitioner's energy along with the patient's energy along with energy available to us from outside ourselves works to bring balance and peace and healing.[17] Healing touch can be performed with hands touching the client, or the practitioner's hands can hover over the client, making this therapy available to people who can't or don't like to be touched.

Pranic Healing: This technique involves using breathing exercises to help move energy. There are other kinds of breathing exercises as well. I have one that I like and do before my meditations. It is supposed to keep you healthy and I am proud to announce that I survived this cold season while those immediately around me were dropping like flies. It is not complicated. You take a deep breath for the count of 4, hold that breath for the count of 7 and release the breath through the mouth to the count of 8. All the while holding your tongue where your front teeth meet the roof of your mouth. Andrew Weil prescribes this breathing method and admits to having no idea why it works; but it does.

WHOLE MEDICAL SYSTEMS

Whole medical systems have enriched my life by giving me choices regarding inner/outer balance. These

---

[17] For more information, see Lisa Anselme, Sue Kagel, and Mary O'Neill, eds., *Healing Touch Certificate Program: Level 1* (Lakewood: Healing Beyond Borders, 2010).

systems include Traditional Chinese Medicine, Ayurveda, osteopathy, homeopathy, naturopathy, and Native American, Latin American, and African indigenous practices. In no way am I eliminating the allopathic (Western) model from my personal resources, but I have learned that having access to multiple systems is good for maintaining optimal health. All of these non-Western systems operate on the theory that there is a vital energy that underlies all health. When that energy is out of balance, we become out of balance either physically, emotionally, or spiritually and the symptoms we develop announce this imbalance.

Homeopathy: This approach to healing is based upon the philosophy of vital energy. It was invented in Germany in 1776 by a man named Samuel Christian Hahnemann and is based on the principle that "like cures like." A homeopath regards symptoms as evidence of the body's inner intelligence and prescribes a remedy to stimulate this internal curative process rather than suppress the symptoms. In homeopathic cures, a natural substance (animal, vegetable, or mineral) is diluted and shaken vigorously (or percussed) in 10ccs of distilled water or alcohol; this process is repeated approximately 30 times for low-potency medicines, and more times for higher-potency medicines. Somewhat counterintuitively, a substance that has been diluted and percussed 200 times is *more* potent, not less, than one that has been diluted and percussed 30 times. Obviously the actual original substance is just about gone from the final product. However, it is believed there is a *footprint* of that substance which becomes more powerful with more dilutions and percussions. The final product is usually tiny white beads and the usual dosage is three of these under the tongue. Usually one or two doses does the trick.[18]

I have had three profound experiences with homeopathy. Twenty-one years ago, I had a minor depression during radiation treatments. A friend gave me a homeopathic interview as a gift. Given the choice of what to focus on, I chose my depression. I received a remedy and did not feel depressed again until my sister died. After my sister died, I began to hear a voice that kept telling me how stupid and incompetent I was; I returned to homeopathy and received a remedy of gold from my doctor. That negative voice is gone. And five years ago, after I started school, my anxiety began to spike. I found myself ruminating over deadlines... *not enough time, which should I do first, running out of time, I'll never get these done on time.* I took a remedy once a week for three weeks, and the voice stopped. Since then, apart from normal stress over deadlines, I have been fine. These remedies absolutely altered my consciousness.

A word of caution. Make sure you find a well-trained practitioner who is properly certified. This is a complete medical system and requires years of training to practice effectively.

Chinese Medicine: Chinese medicine works by

---

[18] Ballentine includes a discussion of homeopathy in *Radical Healing.*

maintaining a balance between the opposite energies of *yin* and *yang* by using diet, herbs, acupuncture, massage, and energy practices such as qigong or tai chi. Acupuncture has become a regular part of my health regime.

Naturopathy: Naturopathy is a system of medicine based upon the healing power of nature. The aim of naturopathy is to support the body's ability to heal itself through the use of dietary and lifestyle changes, herbal medicine, and detoxification. Naturopathic doctors (NDs) treat the whole person, assessing the person's mental, emotional, and spiritual state; diet; family history; environment; and lifestyle before making a diagnosis.[19] My naturopathic doctor is usually my first stop. If she cannot help then I move on to other medical treatment.

Ayurvedic Medicine: This ancient Indian medical system works with the body's constitution (*prakriti*), and life force (*doshas*). Ayurvedic treatment is individualized to each person's constitution. I have not engaged with this approach, however, because I have a difficult time placing myself within categories (I always am very aware of the ways in which I seem to be a different category, or even multiple categories). So even though I test as one type I cannot simply let go and engage with practices for that type because I continually question the assumption that this is the right category for me.

---

[19] See Thornton, *Whole Person Caring*, 16.

CREATIVE/RITUAL PRACTICES

A few other practices are frequently discussed in readings about consciousness, though for years I saw them as not really relevant. But in fact, they are very important.

Creativity: This is a word that I do not like. I am surrounded by artists and my walls are covered in original art. But for years I balked when authors said that we are all creative and need to express our creativity. My mother was creative. She could paint beautifully and also knitted, sewed, crocheted and covered lampshades. She made drapes and curtains, and she had sketch books filled with drawings of hands (which she said were very difficult to draw). I never considered myself to be a creative person. I knit but that is about all. But as I read more I realized that my concept of creativity was stunted. Schlitz talks about creativity as not limited to making art, but as *taking action*.

It can be creative expression, putting your realizations—which can often be difficult to describe—into poetry, drawing, painting, sculpture, or dance. It can be creating new ways of being and spending time with your loved ones. It can be implementing new projects at work—or new elements of existing projects—that are in greater alignment with your emerging values and sensibilities. It can be volunteering in your local community or in broader social or ecological action groups. The bottom line here is bringing your new perspective into the world in some form.[20]

---

[20] Schlitz, Vieten, and Amorok, *Living Deeply*, 146.

From this perspective I am able to see myself as a very creative person. It is just a question of looking at my life through that lens. I have helped heal a fractured family which is extremely creative work. I have written two books. I am constantly figuring ways to re-invent my marriage, looking deeply into myself and finding ways to manifest the qualities I find.

Forgiveness: Forgiveness is one of those words we think we understand, but it is complicated and deserves a lot of conversation. It is something everyone needs to address. Every one of us has been betrayed by someone at some time, or treated badly enough that we cannot shake it. We all have thorns in our sides, sometimes for a long time. It has been said that holding someone in contempt is like drinking poison and thinking it is going to harm the offender. This kind of long-lingering hostility is bad for you—and if you find you cannot forgive you need to find the reason why. For me, the need to be right was a big obstacle to forgiveness. I was right that this person had taken advantage of me and I was stuck on being right. Once I was able to see that, and how foolish it was, I was able to let it go. Being right was far less important than arriving at a neutral stance concerning that person. It is important to note that forgiveness includes self-forgiveness which is often more difficult than forgiving others. For me, it is all about baby steps. There are books on forgiveness and drills that help move in that direction.

Dreamwork: Dreams give us images, symbols, and

storylines straight from our unconscious. There are many systems of dream interpretation, and any connection to dream life can be a valuable component of spiritual practice. I am not a good dream analyzer. I feel the dream so strongly that I cannot see its symbolic nature: I have trouble seeing the forest for the trees. Still, even if you cannot derive good meaning from a dream, just remembering it, writing it down, and listing the symbols and the emotions they inspired is a way of connecting. It does not seem to matter that your brain has difficulty unpacking the dream; just conversing with it and its parts is beneficial to creating and sustaining that connection with the spiritual. Even if you usually do not remember your dreams, there are effective techniques that can help.

Rituals, traditions, and ceremony: This is not a book about traditional religion. It is not even a book about religion; it is a book about the development of a personal theology. That said, I do not want to underestimate the value of ritual, tradition, and ceremony. These activities connect us with other people and spiritual traditions, linking us soul-to-soul. Such connections are why my tears rise whenever I enter a house of worship.

Not all rituals take place in a church or other house of worship, and not all of them are religious. On Thanksgiving I always get together with my children, my grandchildren, my ex-husband, and his wife. It is *our holiday*. We go around the table and say what we are thankful for. This deeply personal and moving ritual usually brings at least one or two people to tears. This tradition has brought great closeness to a family with many fractures.

Teachers: It took me a long time to recognize that teachers are also a path to spiritual connection, possibly because I have a strong disciple archetype and am always studying at the feet of someone. It is second nature to me. The shadow side of that particular archetype is becoming overly attached to a teacher, and staying too long, which is what happened to me in my cult. But now I have many teachers; I see them all around me, and I learn from them and move on with ease.

This is only an incomplete overview of the wide range of practices out there. You have lots of choices. More important, having such choices can be transformative. Five years ago, years after my second cancer diagnosis I was reading Rudolph Ballentine's book *Radical Healing,* and I was fascinated by the array of treatments, remedies, interventions, and practices that I knew little about. While I knew I would gravitate to Western medicine for healing because that was the system I was most familiar with, I wanted to be better informed so that I would have more choices. Learning about the range of options available has left me better informed, and I have built a network of practitioners of exceptional talent, wisdom, and expertise— including both western medicine and complementary practices.

Best of all, I have developed the *intuition* needed to make correct choices. In fact, enhanced intuition is one of the most glorious side effects of this journey of mine.

INTUITION

If there is one aspect of my life that these practices have influenced more than any other it is the development, feeding, nurturing, and expansion of intuition.

Wolfgang Pauli (1900–1958) speaks of intuition or intuitive knowing, which is the opposite of symbolic knowing. Wilber describes this intuition as consisting of "primeval images" that exist outside of rationality—these are "forms belonging to the unconscious region of the human soul, images of powerful emotional content, which are not thought but are beheld, as it were, pictorially."[21]

I love this explanation because it describes what happens to me so poetically and scholastically. My arm is presently talking to me. I think it is an old injury. My left hip has been diagnosed with a small amount of pre-osteoporosis and since the diagnosis I can feel a small tug on that hip as I walk. I think it is time to try Feldenkrais (a therapy involving tiny movements to correct physical imbalances). In the past I have not resonated with this intervention, although my husband raves about it. But right now it feels right. And if past experience is any example, it will be. At this point I just seem to know intuitively how to find relief most of the time. I don't know how this information comes to me but I am guessing that as I open to greater ways of knowing something within me, perhaps ancient wisdom of

---

[21] Wilber, *Quantum Questions*, 170.

some sort comes through.

I'm guessing that my embrace of mystery has moved me in this direction. Mystery moves us toward intuition. As Einstein said, "The only real valuable thing is intuition. Intuition leads us into new territory, allowing us to play with new ideas from which magnificent breakthroughs can develop. If at first an idea is not absurd, then there is no hope for it."[22] And who am I to doubt Einstein?

Intuition has its shadow side as well, as do all things. With the joy of discovery also comes the stab of loss and rejection. In our scientific, secular, anti-woo-woo culture intuition is often scoffed at (some people label anything they cannot quantify "woo-woo"). "But how do you know?" they ask. The answer, "I just do," will simply not suffice in many circles. Sometimes something you know to be true and helpful will be rejected because you cannot *prove* it. I knew that my granddaughter had asthma. I could practically smell it. It took six years before a doctor would give her an official diagnosis of asthma. This made me sad. It is never fun to have a theory rejected that you know would relieve suffering. So prepare yourself.

Gary Zukav in *Seat of the Soul* says that intuition is a message from the soul. And I will add that as a keen observer in my own development of intuition I have found a key. As I find balance, homeostasis, easy connection between my body, mind, spirit, soul, ego, personality, and heart, my intuition flourishes.

---

[22] Blanchard, *Ancient Ways*, 83.

CHAPTER NINE

CAN PRAYER HELP YOU CONNECT
WITH A TRANSCENDENT GOD?

This chapter brings me to my present (most probably temporary) conclusions about God. Many things happened for me during the five years that I studied Spirituality and Holistic Health. I started with several underlying assumptions. One of them was that I didn't know what I thought I knew and I had a wobbly spiritual connection. Now my head is filled with new thoughts and ideas and the chatter that used to fill my mind seems to have taken a firm back seat to discovery. My spiritual connection is strong and steady, giving me choices and options I didn't have before. Many of the new ideas and concepts I am exploring are still pretty blurry. But they will become clear just as forgiveness and creativity have become clearer to me. And finally I have moved on from my vision of God as a white man in the sky with long white hair. Surprisingly it was prayer that moved me to a new place.

Many years ago I listened to a workshop given by Caroline Myss on meditation and prayer. Two questions she asked were important in leading me to expanding my notion of God. The questions were: *Who do you pray to?* and *What do you pray for?* I could not get those questions out of my head and gradually realized that if I was able to answer them I might just begin the process of making God bigger. For that was my problem: my anthropomorphic God was too small.

Anthropomorphizing God is not a bad thing. Allopathic medicine is not a bad thing. Both are simply incomplete systems of belief and practice. In *A History of God*, Karen Armstrong states that when people personalize unseen forces they are expressing their sense of affinity with the unseen, and she sees atheism as a denial of a God no longer adequate to the problems of our time. Similarly, in *The Future of God*, Chopra admonishes writers who demolish God without seriously considering that a father in the sky might not be the only way to think about the divine. There is an alternative to God the Father. I accepted that my version of God was limited, and I desired to expand this version. But I had no idea of how to do that.

Who do you pray to? What do you pray for? I had no idea who I was praying to—some rejected man in the sky? But I at least had a clue about what I was *not* praying for. I was not praying for a new shiny BMW. I knew better than to pray for someone to live if they were dying. I had already decided that even if God existed as a man in the sky, he wasn't focused on making the decisions I wanted, like letting my sister recover and live. I knew that was a fantasy; even more, I understood the arrogance of it. I place more importance on my sister's life than on that of an anonymous 24-year-old soldier fighting in the Middle East, but I certainly could not ask that God do so as well. Still, I began creating prayers. They were crude, immature, poorly worded, but they were a start. And they usually included the words *help me*. This was an excellent start. What I was doing, without consciously realizing it, was trying to climb Chopra's ladder to a level where I would be a co-creator with God. But I still did not have any idea what this God looked like until I read Reverend Linda Martella-Whitsett of the Unity Church.

Martella-Whitsett is a leader in a progressive part of the Unity Church, dedicated to promoting the idea of God dwelling within us. The name of her book is telling: *How to Pray Without Talking to God: Moment by Moment, Choice by Choice*. The following prayers resulted from her experience with her son who, when he reached the age of seventeen, told his mother that he was leaving the church. He said that he was turned off by the prayers that did not reflect the way he related to God. He told her that she taught that God was within, but the prayers said something else. In response she framed her prayers differently, moving away from anthropomorphic theology. Here are two versions of the same prayer, the first written in anthropomorphic language, and following, a modernized version.

The light of God surrounds me

The love of God enfolds me

The power of God protects me
The Presence of God Watches over me
Wherever I Am, God is.

We are here to glow as the Light of God. We are the light of God.

We are here to embrace as the love of God. We are the Love of God.

We are here to stand in Truth as the Power of God. We are the Power of God.

We are here to radiate as the Presence of God. We are the Presence of God.

Wherever we are, God is. And so it is.[1]

This was a departure from the prayers I had been reading in other books, most of which seemed rooted in a belief of human inferiority. One book suggested prayers for everything from the common cold to heart failure, but also gave reasons for the disability in terms of a faulty relationship to God. Many prayers declared man to be grossly inferior to God. These did not work for me, not because I think I'm so great, but because I don't think I'm so small. But as I eliminated them, I came to prayers that do work. I began to produce prayers that did not conjure up the picture of a man in the sky. Following is a discussion

[1] Linda Martella-Whitsett, *How to Pray Without Talking to God: Moment by Moment, Choice by Choice* (Charlottesville: Hampton Roads, 2011), 69.

of prayers that do work, but the short version is that they do not include asking for something from someone who is listening to you and billions of others.

And why was prayer so important? I do not see much difference between prayer and intention. Prayer connects you to divinity, whatever your particular divinity looks like. Intention focuses your desires, wishes, conflicts, pain, and longings. Through prayer you can answer big questions such as *Why am I here? What is my purpose? What am I supposed to be doing?* Intention or prayer forces you to say what you have to say clearly.

After I had sorted much of this out I found a little book by Anne Lamott. Her work is not scholarly, but she is terrifically funny, and a great writer. She became very religious a few years ago and then incorporated her religion back into her life as a writer. In her book called *Help, Thanks, Wow* she says these three words are the only three prayers. And although Lamott is not a scholar in the traditional sense of the word, being able to distill something so large into something so profound puts her way up on my list of brilliance. And so my prayers have become simple. Often they are requests for *help*:

Help me understand why…

Help me see what I'm not seeing…

Help me get this doctoral project organized so I can begin writing…

Help me be kind to this annoying person or that annoying person…

Help me overcome my anger toward....

My *thank yous* are endless. Every night, I sink my head into my sweet-smelling pillow and thank my good fortune for having such a wonderful bed and room to sleep in, and look for one or two more in addition. Since a very good friend had a debilitating stroke, my *thank yous* have become smaller and smaller.

Thank you for my having two hands that work.
Thank you for children who are fully functioning adults.
Thank you for enough to eat.
Thank you for my husband and dogs.

For me *WOW* often goes along with *thank you.* Having two hands that work may not seem like much of a *WOW*, but when your friend has an arm that her brain doesn't even recognize as being there, it becomes one. I see the ocean every single day and that is still a major *WOW.* My husband and I sit down every single evening with a martini and snacks and really talk, sharing our lives on every level— that is also a big *WOW.*

I am not going to try to pretend that I don't have my dark moments. I sometimes feel the stab of hopelessness that I am never going to get through whatever it is I am grappling with. But I always do get to the other side. And my prayers are answered. Not necessarily immediately, and sometimes so surprisingly that I don't even recognize the answers. (One such surprise was that *Theology* is my path—who knew!?) I have learned that this journey toward spirit is not a linear experience and that answers come in many forms. In my own personal case, I can become rigid enough to reject answers because they do not fit the image I hold of myself. I've wasted a lot of time mucking around in areas that are not right for me, but as I move more and more into the life I am supposed to be living, I am finding more and more of the answers I seek.

And then a teacher asked me a question that took me to the finish line: *How can you pray to an abstract God?* I was back with the question of *Who or what do I pray to?* And I think I am at the very beginning of being able to answer that question now.

People I know, who believe in a higher power of some sort but do not believe in a man in the sky, skirt the issue of God. They use words such as *source,* or *field,* or *energy,* or *the universe.* My immediate reaction is: *You mean God, why not say God?* I know why they don't—they know as do I that the man in the sky is bound to become the elephant in the middle of what might be a great conversation about spirituality.

Although there is much food for thought here, let us simply take away that there is something that surrounds us, an energy that is huge and that exists outside of time and space. This thought allows the picture of a man in the sky to gently slip away for me. It has been replaced with something much bigger, which was my goal. Schopenhauer's philosophy states that "under the individual consciousness is a cosmic consciousness, which for the most part is 'unconscious', but which can be awakened and fully realized, and this making conscious of the unconscious was men and women's greatest good."[2] I interpret this to mean that tapping into cosmic consciousness and taking conscious bits and pieces from that cosmic consciousness is a good thing.

You can find much discussion about whether there even is an "outside" consciousness claiming that all consciousness dwells within. I do believe there is an "out there"—I'm not ready to move in the direction of "all is within." And more and more, I am coming to the realization that the "out there" consciousness is God. Chopra says that your brain is hardwired to find God and until you do you will not know who you are. He goes on to say that life looks meaningless when you have old responses, old realities, and old versions of God. In order to find God and give our lives meaning we have to follow new, even strange responses wherever they lead us. The material world won't provide that meaning: in the words of one of Chopra's spiritual teachers, the material world is infinite, but it is a *boring* infinity. The really interesting infinity lies beyond. God is another name for that interesting infinite intelligence. To achieve anything in life, a piece of this intelligence must be contacted and used. In other words God is always there for you.[3]

Others may pray for and long for different things than

---

[2] Ken Wilber, ed., *Integral Psychology: Consciousness, Spirit, Psychology, Therapy* (Boston: Shambhala Publications, 2000), 154.

[3] Deepak Chopra, "7 Levels to God," *Healthy Living* (blog), *Care2*, June 22, 2012, https://www.care2.com/greenliving/seven-levels-to-god.html/.

I do, but this speaks to my desires. When I am in trouble, confused, in crisis, feeling alone and perhaps hopeless, I want answers. What am I not seeing, hearing, feeling? Why am I so confused? If I can tap into infinite intelligence I can get the answers I need and move forward.

After all of this—years of study, papers and deadlines, continued struggle to transform the man in the sky to something larger—I am beginning to see God as Consciousness. This is where all possibility dwells. All I have to do is focus, make my intentions clear mostly to myself, and the answers seem to be readily available. The big problem is my own focus, in keeping my intentions pure and clear. That takes some doing, thus my practices that keep me honest. Consciousness likes honesty. At least in my experience it does.

This seems anti-climactic. All of that work for a solution that feels so simple! But that is what genius is: taking what is incredibly complicated and getting to the simplicity of it. My husband calls it "Picasso simple": drawing a single line that conveys a woman's body. I like to call it the "irreducible truth." This is when you just know that there is no other place to go—you've arrived at the essence of the situation. In the words of Deepak Chopra, "Truth isn't found in words but through insight and self-discovery. Truth isn't taught or earned. It is wrapped inside consciousness itself. Your consciousness must deepen until what is false has been left behind. Then truth will exist by itself, strong and self-sufficient."[4]

---

[4] Chopra, *The Future of God*, 116.

CHAPTER TEN

CONSPICUOUSLY ABSENT: RELIGION, PROOF AND MORALITY

People who read books about finding God usually expect to hear about religion, proof, morality and ethics.

I just don't seem to have the gene for following a religion. I do love religion, but I seem to love all of them. As I was reading about world faiths, from Judaism and Christianity to the Yoruba Orishas or the Tao, each one called to me with equal power. I was fascinated by how different cultures found ways to solve the questions of mystery and what is not knowable through our senses.

What I do not love is doctrine. As I have said, I am a pragmatist and believe in Holism above all. I am always looking for the union that underlies division— and at bottom, religious doctrines are divisive. Each one maintains that my religion is truer, more authentic, more biblical, more ethical, more interesting, just plain *better* than yours. My God is true. Your God is false. And always the underlying assumption is that what we reject is bad, or at best lesser. My mother used to say, "We don't believe in Jesus." My developing brain translated that as: "Jesus is not a good thing—and by extension people who worship Jesus are not a good thing." I cannot escape the fact that unspeakable violence and destruction have been wrought in the name of one religion over another.

And yet religion also can provide ceremony, ritual, and tradition—and these have been lacking in my life. The more my spiritual connection strengthens, the more I long for a community to share this energy with. Having lived in community for so long, I totally understand the power of a group of people experiencing the same thing. I'm not sure this will find resolution.

Proof is another notion that I think just stops good conversation about religion, spirit and God. Conversation can reach a dead end when the conversation turns to whether or not either religious, spiritual or beliefs in God can be proven. I skirt this issue entirely. I see little point in trying to prove the existence of a higher power, I'd much rather continue to strengthen this relationship I now have than *prove* it is real. As Karen Armstrong says, "The experience of God is subjective and it does not seem to be of value to pursue making this otherwise. God was not an external, objective fact but an essentially subjective and personal enlightenment." Armstrong also tells us that we strive to explain, understand and know God in the same way and with the same tools we use to apprehend the known world, noting, "We cannot use reason and language and intellect to find or understand God. We can employ those things to help us experience God, but not understand God."[1] In other words we cannot use the language of the senses to understand and explore the experience of spirit.

Physicist Sir Arthur Eddington puts it in words that resonate with me.

We are haunted by the word *reality*. I have already tried to deal with the questions which arise as to the meaning of reality, but it presses on us so persistently that, at the risk of repetition, I must consider it once more from the standpoint of religion. A compromise of illusion and reality may be all very well in our attitude toward physical surroundings, but to admit such a compromise into religion would seem to be a trifling with sacred things. Reality seems to concern religious beliefs much more than any others. No one bothers as to whether there is a reality behind humour. The artist who tries to bring out the soul in his picture does not really care whether and in what sense the soul can be said to exist. Even the physicist is unconcerned as to whether atoms or electrons really exist; he usually asserts that they do, but, as we have seen, existence is there used in a domestic sense and no inquiry is made as to whether it is more than a conventional term. In most subjects (perhaps not excluding philosophy), it seems sufficient to agree on the things that we shall call real, and afterward try to discover what we mean by the word. And so it comes about that religion seems to be the one field of inquiry in which the question of reality and existence is treated as of serious

---

[1] Armstrong, *A History of God*, 224, 7.

and vital importance.[2]

This last is important to me. We see that Eddington uses the word *religion* as I would use the word *spirituality*, but I think this is because of both when this was written and perhaps because of language translation. He also uses the word reality, which I have omitted from this book because since everyone's reality is unique I prefer to use the word experience. In any case, why we need to prove the existence of higher power remains a big question and I'd much rather have conversation about how to strengthen connection to spirit than to prove that it is real.

Morality: And finally, once God is no longer the man in the sky, this question of God as a regulator of morality pretty much goes away, because we eliminate a God judging good and bad behavior. Even if there were a God in the sky, I don't think he would really get involved with specific behaviors among his people. And even if he did, it doesn't seem to be having much impact. Even though the vast majority of people worldwide believe in God and practice some kind of religion or spirituality our jails remain full and war is rampant. I certainly do not think Consciousness concerns itself with how humans behave. We are free to behave as we wish. So to this Holistic Pragmatist tying our moral behavior to the commandments of a God would be meaningless. But smarter people than I have weighed in on this.

My sense of morality follows a similar line as my sense

---

[2] Wilber, *Quantum Questions*, 211.

of religion: ultimately all the doctrines come down to the same basic thing. As Chopra puts it:

Inner transformation doesn't depend on Buddhism and right doctrine. The same promise was held out by the Vedic sages who lived long before Buddha; by Socrates, who was born soon after Buddha died; and by Jesus five hundred years later. Each opened up the pathless path using different words. When you reach higher consciousness by any means, you no longer separate what is good for you from what is good for everyone.[3]

In *Reinventing the Body*, Chopra tells of a Guru who said that finding God is a hundred times easier than trying to be good. God is part of you, and once you locate that part, being good comes naturally. So when considering whether my actions are moral, I ask myself if I am following the fundamental spiritual laws. If I am following them, then my morality and ethics will be sound. Fundamental spiritual laws can be stated esoterically, but for me, what goes around comes around, we are all connected as in all is one, the truth will set you free, the golden rule and many more are spiritual laws.

When I'm not being true to those laws, I feel the imbalance. This divisiveness I feel around politics in these days of Trump informs me that I am "off" in my quest for holism at least in that particular arena. I am not close to following the rule that all is one on this particular issue. And yet, even divisiveness may be seen as part of God in

---

[3] Chopra, *The Future of God*, 118.

one way or another. Rabbi Larry Kushner says that, "All our behavior is God. Some is very close to God and some is excruciatingly distant." If evil is the absence of light, as Zukav suggests, you are required to examine the choices that you make each moment in terms of whether they move you toward Light or away from it.[4] This is really brilliant and actually shows us the way forward. I don't have to constantly grapple with ethics and morality by focusing on rules and specifics. I simply have to seek connection, ask for help or guidance, and if I keep the connection open the answers will come.

---

[4] Zukav, *The Seat of the Soul*, 47.

CHAPTER ELEVEN

CONCLUSION

For over a year, I have been struggling with a quandary: How am I going to pull all that I have learned together and explain it coherently? And how am I going to move my relationship with God from one that centers on a man in the sky to something bigger? I may not receive rewards for this endeavor, but the reward of knowing what I now know both about God and myself is big.

I seem to have come a long way in my image of the Man in the Sky. Now when I think of him I see something very different from the robed man on the throne. He is an oldish man, perhaps 70 or so, with white cropped hair, khaki pants and a blue button-down shirt. I have no idea where he came from, but his evocation causes me to both laugh and say a big WOW! He is so diminished that I have no choice but to reject him—and how appropriate that I reject him with a laugh!

In his place I have a new theology—one that is closest to the one expressed in Einstein's mysticism:

...a cross between Spinoza and Pythagoras; there is a

central order to the cosmos, an order that can be directly apprehended by the soul in mystical union. He devoutly believed that although science, religion, art, and ethics are necessarily distinct endeavors, it is wonderment in the face of "the Mystery of the Sublime" that properly motivates them all.[1]

And finally, I hope that my journey will be helpful to more than just me. Scientist Louis De Broglie (1892–1987) describes the growth of scientific discoveries that have made us more and more powerful. But, he says, our souls have not grown in proportion to our power: "Now in this excessively enlarged body, the spirit remains what it was, too small now to fill it, too feeble to direct it." If we are going to survive, he says,

...man has need of a "supplement of soul" and he must force himself to acquire it promptly before it is too late. It is the duty of those who have the mission of being the spiritual or intellectual guides of humanity to labour to awaken in it this supplement of the soul.[2]

I feel honored to share my own journey, and I hope that doing so will help support this campaign to enlarge the human spirit.

---

[1] Wilber, *Quantum Questions*, 102.
[2] Wilber, *Quantum Questions*, 126, 129.

Awakening to God
Not a Man in the Sky

Transcending the Ultimate Patriarchy

References and Bibliography

Anselme, Lisa, Sue Kagel, and May O'Neill, eds. *Healing Touch Certificate Program: Level 1.* Lakewood: Healing Beyond Borders, 2010.

Armstrong, Karen. *A History of God: The 4000-Year Quest of Judaism, Christianity and Islam,* New York: Ballantine, 1993.

Ballentine, Rudolph. *Radical Healing,* Honesdale: Himalayan Institute, 2011.

Blanchard, Geral. *Ancient Ways: Indigenous Healing Innovations for the 21st Century,* Holyoke: Neari Press, 2011.

Braden, Gregg. *The Spontaneous Healing of Belief: Shattering the Paradigm of False Limits.* Carlsbad: Hay House, 2009.

Chopra, Deepak. *The Chopra Center* (blog). http://chopra.com/.

———. *The Future of God: A Practical Approach to Spirituality for Our Times.* Nevada City: Harmony Books, 2015.

————. *How To Know God,* New York: Three Rivers Press, 2001.

————. *Reinventing the Body, Resurrecting the Soul,* New York: Three Rivers Press, 2010.

————. "7 Levels to God." *Healthy Living* (blog). *Care2,* June 22, 2012. https://www.care2.com/greenliving/seven-levels-to-god.html/.

————. *Spiritual Solutions: Answers to Life's Greatest Challenges.* New York: Harmony Books, 2012.

Choi, Charles Q. "Peace of Mind! Near-Death Experiences Now Found to Have Scientific Explanations." *Scientific American,* September 12, 2011. https://www.scientificamerican.com/article/peace-of-mind-near-death/.

Corcoran, David, ed. *The New York Times Book of Science: More Than 150 Years of Groundbreaking Scientific Coverage.* New York: Sterling, 2015.

Edwards, Tilden. *Spiritual Director, Spiritual Companion: Guide to Tending the Soul.* New York: Paulist Press, 2001.

Eliade, Mircea. *From Primitives to Zen: A Thematic Sourcebook on the History of Religions.* New York: Harper & Row, 1967.

Grof, Stanislav. *The Cosmic Game: Explorations of the Frontiers of Human Consciousness.* New York: State University of New York Press, 1998.

Hoffman, Louis. "Premodernism, Modernism, and Postmodernism: An Overview." *Postmodern Psychology,* March 14, 2017. http://postmodernpsychology.com/ premodernism-modernism-postmodernism-an-overview/.

Khan, Hazrat Inayat. *Spiritual Dimensions of Psychology,* New Lebanon: Omega Publications, 2012.

Lamott, Anne. *Help, Thanks, Wow.* New York: Riverhead Books, 2012.

Lipton, Bruce. *The Biology of Belief: Unleashing the Power of Consciousness, Matter, and Miracles.* Carlsbad: Hay House, 2015.

Martella-Whitsett, Linda, Rev. *How to Pray Without Talking to God: Moment by Moment, Choice by Choice.* Charlottesville: Hampton Roads, 2011.

Millman, Dan. *The Laws of Spirit: A Tale of Transformation.* Tiburon: New World Library, 1995.

Moore, Thomas. *Care of the Soul: A Guide for Cultivating Depth and Sacredness in Everyday Life.* New York: Harper, 1995.

National Qigong Association. "What is Qigong?" https:// www.nqa.org/what-is-qigong-/.

Naparstek, Belleruth. *Invisible Heroes: Survivors of Trauma and How they Heal.* New York: Bantam House, 2004.

Nordqvist, Joseph. "What are the Health Benefits of Tai Chi?" *Medical News Today*, September 16, 2016, www. medicalnewstoday.com/articles/265507.php/.

Norris, Patricia & Barrett Porter. *Why Me? Harnessing the Healing Power of the Human Spirit.* Walpole: Stillpoint Publishing, 1985.

Pert, Candace. *Everything You Need to Know to Feel Go(o)d.* Carlsbad: Hay House, 2007.

Pearce, Joseph Chilton. *The Biology of Transcendence: A Blueprint of the Human Spirit.* Rochester: Park Street Press, 2002.

Remen, Naomi Rachel. *Kitchen Table Wisdom: Stories that Heal.* New York: Penguin, 2010.

Schlitz, Marilyn, Cassandra Vieten, and Tina Amorok. *Living Deeply: The Art & Science of Transformation in Everyday Life.* Oakland: New Harbinger Publications, 2008.

Schumacher, Lauren. "Newtonian Principles of the Heart." *Huffington Post*, January 13, 2013. https://www. huffingtonpost.com/lauren-schuhmacher/newtonian-principles-of-t_b_2124229.html/.

Thornton, Lucia. *Whole Person Caring: An Interprofessional Model for Healing and Wellness.* Indianapolis: Sigma Theta Tau International, 2013.

Thoresen, Carl E. and Alex H.S. Harris. "Spirituality and Health: What's the Evidence and What's Needed?" *Annals of Behavioral Medicine* 24, no. 1 (2002): 3-13.

Tick, Edward. *War and the Soul: Healing Our Nation's Veterans from Post-traumatic Stress Disorder.* Wheaton: Quest Books, 2005.

Tiller, William A. *Science and Human Transformation: Subtle Energies, Intentionality and Consciousness.* Walnut Creek, Pavior Publishing, 1997.

Tolle, Eckhart. *A New Earth: Awakening to Your Life's Purpose.* New York: Penguin, 2008.

Wade, Jenny. *Changes of Mind: A Holonomic Theory of the Evolution of Consciousness.* Albany: State University of New York Press, 1996.

Walsh, Roger, and Frances Vaughan, eds. *Paths Beyond Ego: The Transpersonal Vision.* New York, Penguin, 1993.

Walsh, Roger N. *The Spirit of Shamanism.* New York: Perigee Books, 1990.

Wilber, Ken, ed. *Quantum Questions: Mystical Writings of the World's Greatest Physicists.* Boston, Shambhala Publications, 2000.

Wilber, Ken, ed. *Integral Psychology: Consciousness, Spirit, Psychology, Therapy.* Boston: Shambhala Publications, 2000.

Woodman, Marion. *The Crown of Age: The Rewards of Conscious Aging*. Read by the author. Sounds True Audio, 2004.

Zukav, Gary. *The Seat of the Soul: A Remarkable Treatment of Thought, Evolution, and Reincarnation*. New York, Simon & Schuster, 1989.

About the Author

ALICE ROST

Spiritual seeker, teacher, and devoted disciple, Alice Rost has been committed to transformation for over 50 years and feels like she is just getting started at 75 years old.

As a mother, grandmother, wife, and sister to many, Alice knows the importance of giving and receiving support. As a successful business owner with her husband who together built a thriving and dynamic business, she knows the power of partnerships.

Exquisite self-care and her spiritual practice carried her through two cancers, which she claims are "quiet" while she lives a robust life.

The call of spirit along with her thirst for knowledge sent her back to graduate school as a well-established senior and earned her a degree in Spirituality and Holistic Health with a specialty in Transpersonal Psychology.

With so much life experience, energy comparable to a 30 year old, and a reclamation as a mystic and wise woman, Alice is on a mission to teach groups of women how to embrace their feminine power through Sistership Circles.

She believes that by balancing the male and female energies within themselves, women will bring the balance of these powers into the world.

CPSIA information can be obtained
at www.ICGtesting.com
Printed in the USA
FSHW02n0802050818
51172FS